Bridal Fashions

Little bridal attendants./*Gazette du Bon Ton*

Bridal Fashions

by Pauline Stevenson

Left: **In May 1970 a bridal archway of flowers was formed at St Tropez for Michel Raimon, son of Alexandre, the hairdresser, and Evelyne de Beschart.** /*Keystone Press*

Right: **Dress by Lanvin in the twenties.**/*Femina*

LONDON

IAN ALLAN LTD

First published 1978

ISBN 0 7110 0690 3 (Casebound edition)
ISBN 0 7110 0849 3 (Paperback edition)

Designed by Christopher Cusack.

Published by Ian Allan Ltd, Shepperton, Surrey; and printed in the United Kingdom by Ian Allan Printing Ltd

Above: **A wedding during World War I, 1918. The bridegroom is behind the bride, the wounded soldiers are the bride's brother and the best man. Very pale pink and white were the colour themes and small rosebuds decorated the headdresses of the bridesmaids and the bride's dress. The child bridesmaid wore pink voile and a Florentine straw hat.**

Right: **A 1914 wedding dress in white tulle embroidered in diamanté worn with a veil of Honiton lace, a wreath of orange flowers and myrtle. A white satin cummerbund surrounds the waist, and the train, on which there is a large tulle bow, is edged with orange flowers. The corsage ornament is of orange flowers and white heather. Drawing by P. Stevenson.**

Contents

June 17th 1550.

The wedding clothes of Miss Elizabeth Draper, 1550, a present from her husband, John Bowyer Esq. of Lincoln's Inn:—

Wedyn-apparell bought for my wyffe, Elizabeth Draper, the younger, of Camberwell, against 17 die Junii, anno Domini 1550 with dispensalls.

4 ells of tawney taffeta at 11s 6d the ell, for the Venyce gowne 46s 0d

4 yardes of silk Chamlett crymsyn at 7s 6d the yard 52s 6d

One yard and a half of tawney velvet to gard the Venyce gown, at 15s the yard 22s 6d

Half a yard of crymsyn satin for the fore-slyves 6s 8d

8 yards of russel's black, at 4s 6d the yard, for a Dutch gowne 35s 0d

A yard and a quarter of velvet black, to gard the Dutch gowne 17s 8d

One yard and a quarter of skarlett, for a pety cote with plites 20s 0d

The wedding ring is described as weighing 'two angels and a duckett' graven with these words:
"Deus nos junxit, J.E.B.Y.R."

The date of the wedding is inserted with great minuteness (at the hour of eight, the dominical letter F, the moon being in Leo).

from Hone's everyday book 1827

Introduction

The last 70 years have seen the gradual emancipation of women and many of us now cannot visualise the state of subjection in which they once lived. If today's bride, for instance, could meet some of those of past centuries, both sides would be in for a series of shocks. Today the bride goes willingly to the altar with the man of her choice and her bridal clothes have crystallised into a formal convention; so has the ceremony whether it takes place in a church, chapel or a registry office. Afterwards the married pair depart on their honeymoon, and if things don't turn out happily there is always the divorce court.

In the past — and we are going back now to the Middle Ages — women had no legal rights over their own property after marriage, and often seem to have been handed over by their parents to their husbands like so many parcels of merchandise. Frequently they were betrothed in their cradles and married at 12 or 13 to men very much older, simply because the respective parents or guardians wanted to join various estates together, to get political power, or in the case of royalty, to enlarge their kingdoms. If such women survived into middle life, they had often been married three or four times, to men either much younger or very much older, frequently widowers who in their turn had lost two or three wives in childbirth. Added to this, in the Middle Ages, due to the power of the church and its teaching, women were considered as a necessary evil, the daughters of deceitful Eve, and some clerics — all rigorously celibate themselves — went so far as to describe them as 'The Gates of Hell'.

Ideas of romantic love rarely entered these matrimonial transactions; love often followed the wedding, but no woman took it for granted that she could marry whom she wished as a matter of course. Thus Fanny Burney, a lady-in-waiting to Queen Charlotte, the wife of George III said in her diary of 1789:

'Longleat was formerly the dwelling of the Earl of Lansdowne... and here at this seat, that heartless uncle, to promote some political views, sacrificed his incomparable niece at the age of 17, marrying her to an unwieldy, uncultivated country esquire nearly 60 years of age and scarce ever sober'.

This extract shows that marriages of convenience were still common in the 18th century and in fact were quite usual well into the 19th century. From 1882 onwards, however, a law was passed making it possible at last for a married woman to keep her own property.

Today's bride would also see her mediaeval counterpart being married in the church porch. Not until the ring was safely on did the couple enter the church for the rest of the service. The girl would not necessarily be wearing white. She would be in the best she could afford — either a simple or gaudy dress according to her taste, and in any colour she preferred. Her hair would be hanging down her back as a sign of virginity, and round her head might be a coronet or a little cap decorated with flowers, gilt or lace. Wild flowers were strewn in the path of the country bride together with sprigs of rosemary. Anne of Cleeves married Henry VIII in 1540 in cloth of gold embroidered with pearl flowers, her long golden hair hanging down her back, and around her head a coronet of gold and jewels mixed with small branches of rosemary. The rosemary was often dipped in scented water,

The most exciting part of the wedding was the feasting, dancing, playing and singing that went on after the ceremony, and of course, the ritual of 'putting the bride to bed'. She was undressed by her women relatives and the bridesmaids, who had carefully to extract all the pins from the clothing and throw them away. If this was not done the bride would have very bad luck, and the bridesmaids would not be married as soon as they might wish.

The bride's stockings were kept up by long silken garter ribbons, generally blue, the colour of the Virgin Mary, and for these the groomsmen fought, to put them in their hats. If she did not wish too much fingering and pinching of her legs, the bride would take care to loosen her garters a little first. Once the stockings were off, a kind of game took place; the bridesmaids and groomsmen would sit on the end of the bed with their backs to the married pair throwing them backwards over their shoulders, the bridesmaids trying to hit the bridegroom, and the groomsmen

An early 16th century woodcut by Hans Bucknair showing the dowry being brought to the groom's home./*Mary Evans Picture Library.*

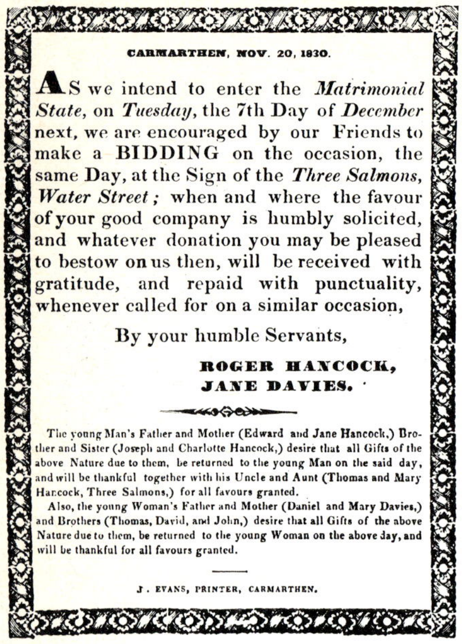
CARMARTHEN, NOV. 20, 1830.

AS we intend to enter the *Matrimonial State*, on *Tuesday*, the 7th Day of *December* next, we are encouraged by our Friends to make a BIDDING on the occasion, the same Day, at the Sign of the *Three Salmons, Water Street;* when and where the favour of your good company is humbly solicited, and whatever donation you may be pleased to bestow on us then, will be received with gratitude, and repaid with punctuality, whenever called for on a similar occasion,

By your humble Servants,

ROGER HANCOCK,
JANE DAVIES.

The young Man's Father and Mother (Edward and Jane Hancock,) Brother and Sister (Joseph and Charlotte Hancock,) desire that all Gifts of the above Nature due to them, be returned to the young Man on the said day, and will be thankful together with his Uncle and Aunt (Thomas and Mary Hancock, Three Salmons,) for all favours granted.

Also, the young Woman's Father and Mother (Daniel and Mary Davies,) and Brothers (Thomas, David, and John,) desire that all Gifts of the above Nature due to them, be returned to the young Woman on the above day, and will be thankful for all favours granted.

J. EVANS, PRINTER, CARMARTHEN.

The bidding./*Mary Evans Picture Library*

attempting to hit the bride. All this was supposed to ensure the success of their own marriages. This game was still played at weddings into the 18th century.

Much money was spent in earlier times on wedding favours. These were gloves, generally scented but not generally fitting, and bunches of ribbon or small bouquets, given by the bride's parents to friends and relatives attending the marriage. This custom was still in use in 1840 at Queen Victoria's wedding, when favours were described as being of all sizes, many of white satin ribbon made into bows with layers of silver lace. Some bouquets of ribbon enclosed small sprigs of orange blossom. The actual holding of flowers in the hand as a bridal bouquet seems to have become customary in the 18th century. Possibly the modern version of the wedding favour is the white carnation worn by the bridegroom, best man and ushers, and often the wedding guests as well. It seems to have been considered unlucky to wear orange blossom on any other occasion than a wedding, but its use at weddings appears to have originated in France in about 1830. Myrtle with its beautiful aromatic scent was also used in wedding wreaths and bouquets, and apparently Queen Victoria was the first English bride to wear it at her own wedding, having some cut from a bush growing at Windsor. Brides in Germany are supposed to have worn it long before Queen Victoria introduced it to England.

Two knives in one sheath were wedding gifts given to brides from the 16th and 17th centuries. Perhaps *two* were lucky, but certainly an old superstition said the giving of a knife had the effect of severing a friendship!

Today we still throw old shoes after the bride and her groom, or attach cans to the back of the honeymoon car. This throwing of shoes is a very old custom and was thought to bring luck to all travellers; it may also signify the passing of authority over the bride from the father to the husband. Confetti nowadays replaces the wheat and rice formerly thrown over the bride and bridegroom as guarantee of fertility, and of course much importance has always been attached to the wedding ring, a symbol of eternity.

Rings were originally exchanged in betrothal ceremonies, and until the 17th century wedding rings were worn on the right hand. Mottoes were engraved inside the ring, such as *Mizpah*, ie, 'The Lord watch between me and thee when we are parted one from another', or 'God alone of two makes one'. The present writer has a betrothal ring made in the 18th century; two gold hands hold a flower and behind the flower and under glass are the entwined hair of the two lovers, one dark and one fair.

During Oliver Cromwell's Commonwealth, jolly weddings were frowned on. Although some weddings took place in church, the wedding couple wore their ordinary clothes and the clergyman had no surplice. The churches had in many cases been badly knocked about by the Roundhead soldiers or were often used by them as stables or storerooms. Broken glass and damaged carving did not make them attractive places in which to be married.

In the 18th century the desire seems to have been for as much privacy as possible, for people were frequently married in their own homes in ordinary clothes. When the short ceremony ended everyone joined in an informal meal and the couple went away, sometimes accompanied by a woman relative. Alternatively, they might simply stay at home or make a short visit to friends not too far away. Travelling after all was then a dangerous business. There were no proper roads, highwaymen lurked on lonely heaths, and most of the inns were not fit places to take a bride.

Towards the end of the 18th century, however, much more attention was paid to the actual wedding ceremony. It was then that the fashion of being married in white with a wreath and veil began.

In the early 19th century there was quite a rage for gold, and gold and white for decorative uses, due perhaps to the Neo-Classical influence then at its height. The fashionable wedding dress picked up the trend and one finds frequent examples of rich satin and silk dresses worn with bonnets and veils in various shades of this colour, varying from a brownish to a bright yellow gold. White was worn for every occasion, in the flimsiest of materials, muslin being one of the most popular fabrics. The unhappy Lady Byron was married in a perfectly simple white muslin dress, high waisted with long sleeves, its only trimming being two rows of finely embroidered muslin around the wrists, hem and neck. For her wedding journey she wore over this a long white silk coat with long twisted silk cords and tassels hanging down from the centre back, and on her hands thin white lace gloves. Nothing could be more child-like in its effect, or more resemble the classical Greek statue to which every fashionable lady aspired.

In terms of fashion, the period from 1800 to 1900 splits up fairly easily into decades. First came the high-waisted, classical, nearly naked look, then, gradually, towards 1825 and 1830, by dint of adding more and more petticoats and trimmings and enlarging the sleeves, arrival at a silhouette nowadays suggestive of a ballet dancer. The waistline dropped to the normal position and the dresses were accompanied by extraordinarily twisted and upstanding hairstyles, huge hats and berets of all types worn dashingly on one side.

Towards 1840 a new demure young lady made her appearance — probably because England had a new young Queen in the seventeen-year-old Victoria. The sloping shoulders of this new model young lady drooped and her skirt resembled an upturned wineglass. She had long ringlets on either side of the face, but these were hidden by her poke bonnet. As the Queen matured, married and became the mother of nine (a fact which she tried to conceal each time as long as possible) the silhouette of the period grew more and more ponderous and rounded, the waist rose again and the bonnet, now much smaller, slipped to the back of the head.

Paeans of praise greeted the invention in 1856 of the crinoline, a wonderful cage-like frame which did away with the need for quantities of bulky petticoats but created the much sought-after rounded silhouette. It displayed, however, some rather unfortunate disadvantages when this cage swung suddenly up at the back or front to reveal to the world at large that knickers, as we understand them, were not invariably worn. One gallant and high-born gentleman was heard to remark that 'the gates of Paradise were always open'. Although the legs were covered by long tubes of cotton embroidered round the ankle, these were usually attached to a tape around the waist and had no back or front; indeed, they were sometimes attached just above the knee.

With the advent of the new Princess of Wales, afterwards Queen Alexandra, who was married in 1863 and who disliked the crinoline, dresses became flatter in front and the fullness was bunched up at the back. This style was at its height in the 1870s. In the 1880s the torso appears like a hard metallic version of Venus rising from the waves; the body has taken on the look of an hour-glass emerging from swathes of elaborately folded material draped round the hip line and billowing into a train behind.

Between 1870 and 1890 various types of bustle were used to create prominent posteriors and the figure was cruelly tight-laced to get the required hour-glass effect. Women even went to bed in their corsets and many died young from the results of these constrictions.

The 1890s were remarkable for the leg-of-mutton sleeve which, by 1895, had swelled out horizontally to suggest balloons in the act of deflating. The skirt formed a triangular shape from the still corsetted body, while the waist returned to its natural position. All these bulky sleeves had disappeared by 1900 but an even more iniquitous corset had made its appearance, which forced the top half of the body forward to a very low and mature-looking bust line, while the *derrière* — as it was politely known — was thrust out at the back. This was certainly the age of the woman in her prime, the woman between 25 and 40, the *femme du monde.* These styles were in vogue during the brief decade when King Edward VII and Queen Alexandra were on the throne; they were a royal couple in the forefront of fashion.

The American-born novelist Henry James wrote of the woman of this period in his book *The Ambassadors*, published in 1903. From that one learns how emancipated the American woman was, even at this early period. In England, too, a new woman was emerging, able to participate in nearly every type of sport, constricting though her clothes seem to us. Back in the 1840s the American, Mrs Amelia Bloomer, had introduced the divided skirt and this now returned to favour with the craze for cycling that was rampant at the end of the century.

Many writers have emphasised the way in which fashion indicates to the world at large what is actually happening in society. With their over-elaborate, over-emphasised shapes, the clothes of the 19th century tell us, even if we had never read the history books, that this period was characterised by an extremely wealthy class of society accustomed to showing off its wealth in every way possible. It was, of course, the newly rich middle class who had made their money almost overnight as a result of the Industrial Revolution, which had disturbed to older, more cultured and restrained landed order. Rich men's wives and daughters attempted to ape the old aristocracy, but lacked the background of generations of breeding, taste and education. We see this same ostentation not only in clothes of the period, but in all aspects of interior decorations and home furnishing — the ugly shapes and harsh colours and the over-elaborate tasteless detail which characterised the middle and late Victorian period. To provide the vast amounts of trimming and decoration of every sort not only on clothes, but on chairs, curtains, blinds — and even piano legs — not only were factories kept busy, but scores of poor women outworkers slaved by candlelight, frequently going blind or dying of consumption in the process.

Many of the old aristocracy had been gradually getting poorer because their property, being in land and estates, was largely entailed. They were looking for rich heiresses and welcomed with open arms the exciting and generally wealthy young ladies from the New World, whose papas had made millions from railways, oil, steel, gold or chemicals.

Conversely there were the South Africans and Australians who had set out penniless for the Colonies and now returned to the Old Country as millionaires to enter the aristocracy by marrying a lady from a titled family. Any title was thought to be deliciously exotic. But the most avid title seekers were those eligible young American women who flocked to Europe on what were ostensibly educational trips, but who in private, one feels, were cherishing visions of notepaper and embroidered sheets decked with coronets, and of being addressed either as 'Your Grace', 'My Lady', 'Duchess' or 'Countess'.

Some of the resulting partnerships turned out very happily. New blood was infused into lineage which had been inpoverished by generations of inter-marriage. Certainly many estates benefited by the dollars brought over under marriage settlements. One such example, though far from happy, was that of the famous Consuelo Vanderbilt who became Duchess of Marlborough, impressing all who saw her by her slimness, upright carriage and extreme elegance.

The wedding dress of Princess (later Queen) Alexandra worn at her marriage to the Prince of Wales, later Edward VII, 1863. Princess Alexandra's dress was of silver tissue and lace with a lace veil. The headdress was of orange flowers, diamonds and the Prince of Wales feathers. The dress, which did not have a crinoline, was a forerunner of the fashions of the 1870s. Drawing by P. Stevenson from a contemporary painting.

Another famous and exciting American beauty, Jenny Jerome, was destined to become the mother of Sir Winston Churchill; her dark good looks and strong personality stand out in many contemporary photographs. She married Lord Randolph Churchill, son of the 6th Duke of Marlborough. From San Francisco came Maude Burke, who, when she married Sir Bache Cunard, the Anglo-Canadian shipping magnate, and came to live at Neville Holt in Leicestershire, characteristically changed her first name to Emerald. A great hostess, leader of fashion and staunch supporter of any worthwhile artistic cause, this wonderful woman, beloved by George Moore the writer for so many years, has been thrillingly described by Cecil Beaton in *The Glass of Fashion*.

After the sewing machine was invented in the middle of the 19th century (at first it was much more popular in America than in England), the home dressmaker came into her own. With the aid of paper patterns provided by the growing number of ladies' magazines, she embarked on what would seem to us extraordinarily elaborate dresses, blouses and other articles of female adornment.

Girls were expected to be good at needlework and so it was not considered remarkable to 'run up a dainty little frock' in a day. This would have a gored skirt and a lined and boned bodice, probably decorations of various sorts, and hooks and eyes or buttons and buttonholes. Wedding dresses were often made at home, either by the bride herself and her mother and sisters, or by a sewing woman who would come in and sit solidly sewing all day long for very little money and a meal. Whole trousseaux could be made that way. The rich employed the court dressmaker, who was clever at adapting the latest Paris fashion for her customers. Across the Atlantic American women were just as fashion-conscious as their European sisters, judging by the massive orders for materials and accessories that were sent to Paris and London. Weddings, like race meetings and Sunday church, were the occasions when the plantation-owner's wife and the women on cattle ranches or farms could get together and show off their latest finery. Weddings, of course, were much the most popular occasions, and every detail of the ceremony and trousseau could be discussed with breathless fascination. Marriages were expected to last for life and so was the trousseau; hence the various articles of underwear and household linen were made or ordered in dozens, or even by the gross, according to status.

Because the American pioneers and settlers would never have achieved what they did without the devotion and strength of mind and body of the women who went with them, women in the New World did not have the same struggle for emancipation as their sisters in Europe. Society in Europe before 1914 was entirely man-dominated and in England there were even a few cases of husbands selling their wives. In 1833, for example, a man auctioned his wife to a dustman in a market, and eleven years later a Yorkshireman sold his wife, described as being about '25 years old and rather good-looking' to a collier named Idle. In each case the crowd were hostile and in the latter incident the husband was arrested, though later discharged; but not so the unfortunate woman — she was charged with bigamy! Several other cases in which the husband took his wife to market as he would have taken a cow with a halter round her neck are cited in a contemporary publication called *The Book of Days*.

As was mentioned earlier, until 1882, when the Married Woman's Property Act was finally passed, a woman on marriage lost all the independence she had enjoyed as a single woman. She forfeited all control over her own property and money and her husband had the right to any money she earned or any gifts she received. If he wished, he could sell her clothes and jewels even after he had left her to live with another woman. He was also entitled under law to will her money to someone else. For a wife to keep any of her property under her own control a special trust had to be created. Not until the 1850s did women unite in sufficient strength to collect 26,000 signatures to put before both Houses of Parliament to seek a fairer deal. Even then it took until 1882 to get recognition of a wife's right to dispose of her own property. Not that this solved the problem — indeed it led frequently to further bitterness and dispute in many marriages as husbands endeavoured to badger, bully and cajole their wives into compliance. Nor was divorce in such circumstances easy. Not only was it a highly expensive process, but there were strong social taboos against the scandal and publicity it inevitably aroused.

Few careers other than marriage were open to women during most of the 19th century. We have only to recall the difficulties encountered by the redoubtable Florence Nightingale in establishing nursing as a proper profession for women. Women could, of course, become governesses, but governesses were considered as a sort of upper servant, badly paid, patronised and a failure in the marriage stakes. In the absence of a personal future, marriage could only be obtained through the fleeting charms of face and figure. No one cared about women's minds — or indeed considered them capable of rational thought at all. This may explain some of the excesses of fashion in the 19th century — the extraordinary corsets, dress improvers (false busts), bustles, crinolines and crinolettes, false hair, flowered and feathered hats, laces, ribbons, parasols and gloves, not to mention the elegant little boots. It was all a frantic attempt to promote sex-appeal and the matrimonial stakes.

Magazines for women — or, rather 'Ladies' — were full of advice, hints, warnings and admonitions on behaviour, etiquette and fashion.

As the century wore on increasing attention was paid to weddings. Women were invited to write for advice on the subject, as this letter from *The Queen* of July 1881 suggests: 'A Quiet Wedding. Will anyone tell me what class of refreshments should be offered to the few guests at a very quiet wedding, where the bride only wears walking dress, and no wedding breakfast is contemplated? Is it usual to have cake? Any information concerning this kind of wedding would be gratefully received. (Signed *Hazy*'.)

The Lady Editress of *Myra's Journal*, 1889, made a series of revealing replies: '*Roseleaf*. The trousseau is only shown to the intimate lady friends; no part of it *whatever* except, perhaps, furs and laces should be exhibited with the presents'.

'*Dulcinea*. Wedding dresses are made with long court trains for which four breadths of material may be allowed; they are of course expensive for they must be made of good materials. As to your second inquiry, we cannot decide the question for you, it appears to be one mainly of cost, and you must be prepared to pay at least 12 guineas for a nice dress, probably more'.

Two things stand out in these early women's magazines. The first is the number of fashions that apparently were made by the home dressmaker through a paper pattern service. The second is that although nearly every woman's object was marriage, very few wedding dresses are actually shown, compared with any other kind of dress and accessory. Not until the very end of the century were even fashionable weddings reported at length, or pictures of them published.

Although most brides of any social standing did expect to have a white wedding, the middle and lower classes very often still wore a coloured dress which was used for Sundays afterwards. It was also considered very forward and immodest for a young lady to wish to draw attention to herself; this may have been one reason for the lack of reportage on weddings.

In the *Age of Innocence* Edith Wharton amusingly describes a fashionable New York wedding in the 1870s. The two mothers-in-law are portrayed like this:

'Mrs Welland came first, on the arm of her eldest son. Her large pink face was appropriately solemn, and her plum-coloured satin with pale blue side panels, and blue ostrich plumes in a small satin bonnet, met with general approval... Mrs Lovell Mingott had the high colour and glassy stare induced in ladies of her age and habit by the effort of getting into a new dress... and it was agreed that her black Chantilly over lilac satin, with a bonnet of Parma violets, formed the happiest contrast to Mrs Welland's blue and plum colour'.

The bride's arrival was concealed by an awning stretching from the carriage to the church porch. Its purpose was to prevent 'an army of dressmakers and newspaper reporters who stood outside fighting to get near the joints in the canvas' from seeing anything. 'Why, they might even take a *photograph* of my child and put it in the papers!' Mrs Welland exclaimed. From such unthinkable indecency the clan recoiled with a collective shudder.

Even the newest dresses from Paris were kept two years after arrival in New York, in a trunk. It was considered bad taste to put them on immediately!

From a contemporary magazine comes the following earnest advice:

The Wife

'Of all those qualities which captivate the heart of man, *modesty* bordering on bashfulness, is, in woman, the most effectual. As the evidence of purity of feeling, it gives the best assurance of happiness in a nearer connection, and gleams with the brightness of a halo round the altar of marriage.

'I will suppose her married to the man of her choice, and the honeymoon already far advanced; and I trust up to this period the many veilings of the foibles of her husband have not stimulated complaint or bickering. Unless the acquaintance has endured for some time, one or two years or more, there *must* be much disguise as to the *real* temper and inclinations on both sides; and when these are shown to be in direct opposition to all former appearances, the shock to the heart of a woman of true sensibility is dreadful indeed! *Forbearance* is her only refuge in such a case — by meekness and amiability, not uncombined with gentle dignity and firmness, she may yet triumph and turn the seeming desert into an Eden'.

Perhaps it was for such reasons of modesty that Queen Victoria, her daughter-in-law Queen Alexandra and her grand-daughter Queen Mary, all important 19th century brides, were married either in the Chapel Royal or at Windsor. Neither they, nor any of Queen Victoria's numerous daughters were married in Westminster Abbey; one was even married in the dining room at Osborne House and another at the small parish church of Whippingham. Presumably weddings were occasions for much blushing and modesty on the part of the bride and hence any publicity was to be shunned. All were, however, married in white with veils, wreaths, and bouquets and their wedding dresses followed the fashion of the time.

Queen Victoria married her adored Albert in 1840 at St James's Palace in white satin with a long white satin train edged with sprays of orange blossom. The dress, with its long pointed bodice, had a full skirt arranged in small pleats all the way round set into the small waistline. The neck was low and revealed the shoulders; a deep bertha of what appears to be Honiton lace fell from the shoulders to the bust line. This lace also formed a

Queen Victoria's wedding bonnet trimmed inside and outside with orange blossom and covered with a lace veil. It was probably worn on her wedding drive to Windsor after the wedding breakfast at Buckingham Palace. Drawing by P. Stevenson./*London Museum*

Queen Victoria in her wedding dress, wreath and orders, 1840.

deep panel on the front of the skirt. The sleeves reached the elbows in a double puff and were trimmed with bows of white ribbon and falling bands or frills of lace.

Victoria's hair was parted in the middle, with two shiny pieces arranged in front of the ears on both sides and a wreath, wide in front and smaller at the back, surrounding her head. At the back was arranged a lace veil, which fell to the knees. Many engravings show her with a large gold chain round her neck and what appears to be a spray of flowers, possibly in the form of a small bouquet-holder, tucked into her corsage. To go away on her wedding trip she apparently wore a wedding bonnet of white, trimmed inside and outside the brim with orange blossom; this had a veil which partly concealed her face. On the eve of the wedding there was a grand ball at Buckingham Palace (Victoria loved dancing) and for this she wore a similar style of dress to her wedding dress, but in white watered silk, or faille; the sleeves and neck were trimmed with silver net and small white satin bows. A deep flounce of silver net also trimmed the skirt, which had white satin bows in front.

When in 1863 the Prince of Wales married Princess Alexandra of Denmark, the Queen was an inconsolable widow and viewed the proceedings in St Geroge's Chapel, Windsor, dressed completely in black except for her widow's cap. An onlooker said he 'was much touched by the spectacle of all the royal princesses [sisters of the bridegroom] who, after all, to them was but their Bertie, in tears behind their bouquets, while Queen Victoria looked heavenwards during the singing of the Chorale (composed by Albert) as if he and she were alone before the throne of God'.

In many respects it must have been a dreary affair for the young couple; it rained, the carriages were shabby and the whole atmosphere suppressed feelings of happiness and gaiety.

The bride, who was noted for her charm and tact, took a great interest in fashion, but she did not wear the popular crinoline which was the rage just then. In fact she wore a dress which accurately forecast the styles of the 1870s. It had a short back-laced bodice marked with belt and short net sleeves. The skirt had no fullness in front, but was gathered at the back into large flat pleats which fell into a long train behind. The dress was of silver tissue with four deep tiers of lace in front decorated on the top of each tier and across the bodice with orange blossom. On her head was a small crown-like creation of flowers, diamonds and the traditional Prince of Wales feathers, from which fell a long lace veil. Eight bridesmaids followed her, charmingly dressed in white tulle in a semi-crinoline style slightly flattened in front and with veils. Roses decorated their skirts and bodices and formed tight wreaths on their heads.

One of the few photographs taken on the day of the wedding is redolent of the atmosphere in which it was solemnised. The bride and bridegroom stand on each side of Queen Victoria, who wears dense black. She seems oblivious of the young people on each side of her and contemplates in deep gloom the bust of Albert on a stand. Alexandra is probably wearing her going-away bonnet of white satin with a high, narrow brim lined with lace and orange blossom, and a tiny crown of white satin, and white satin ribbons and tulle streamers. She seems to be the only one smiling at the photographer and enjoying the occasion. This is perhaps not surprising when one recalls that her childhood and early youth had been spent in the extremely simple and even poor surroundings of one of six children of an insignificant branch of the impoverished Danish Royal family.

The last important Royal bride of the 19th century was Princess May of Teck, known to most of us as Queen Mary, who married the Duke of York, afterwards George V, in 1893. The wedding group shows her surrounded by her ten bridesmaids — five grown-ups and five children. Although the older girls look reserved and rather expressionless, the younger five grouped around the bride's chair and sitting on the floor are all chatting away to each other totally oblivious of the camera. Only one is camera-conscious.

The bride's dress was made at Spitalfields of white satin with a silver interwoven design of roses, shamrocks, thistles and orange flowers. The bodice was laced behind and pointed in front and draped around the low shoulder line with lace, which formed the sleeves.

The white upper skirt was cut in an inverted V-shaped opening in front to show the cream satin underskirt, which was decorated with flounces of white lace. The V-shape was outlined with orange blossom, which also outlined the right side of the bodice. The over skirt was pleated at the back and formed a train which was underlined at the edge with thick silk ruching. The bodice was cut most beautifully (she had a beautiful figure) and the small veil of Honiton lace hanging at the back of the head fell from a tiny flowered cap-like creation on the top of her fashionable, tightly curled hair.

She carried an enormous bouquet from which hung long trails of flowers and long pieces of broad white ribbon. All the materials used in the trousseau were made in Britain. It was a most popular marriage and the streets were hung with roses and other flowers so that everyone seemed to be rejoicing in a flower garden.

Women's magazines of the Edwardian period (1901 to 1910) give us a vivid impression of overdressed, overweight men and well-nourished women taking part in a continuous round of gaiety. Superficial activities such as bazaars, charity dinners, luncheon parties, race meetings, theatres and fashionable weddings appear to have abounded. Weddings are for the first time reported in the minutest detail, with illustrations not only of the bride in her dress and with her bouquet and veil, and of her going-away outfit, her bridesmaids large and small, and pages if any, but also of her mother's dress and quite often the toilettes of fashionable members of society who attended the ceremony. There is a plentiful and rather superfluous scattering of French terms throughout, photographs of the couple before marriage, descriptions of the flowers and music at the church, the presents — invariably described as costly or valuable — the reception and how and where the honeymoon was to be spent. For high society couples this last was generally a rather lengthy wedding trip and it was customary for the first part of the honeymoon to be spent somewhere quiet in the English countryside.

Society weddings appear to have taken place every week in the London season and during the winter months as well. In August, when no one who was anyone was in town, and during the autumn they were often staged in the country church attached to the seat of the bride's parents or one of her relatives.

If an English aristocrat got married in Paris that was reported too, and the fullest details were given of the family history on both sides. A typical report of such a wedding is the description of an American widow's marriage in Paris to an Englishman, Lord Monson, which follows. Note the style of the lady reporter, who signs herself by the unlikely name of Ella de C. Bello. It also demonstrates how the nineteenth century devotion to mourning had disappeared with the death of Queen Victoria.

Fashionable Marriages

'A quiet wedding but one which attracted considerable attention in the diplomatic and social world of Paris was that which took place on Wednesday at the Embassy Church between Lord Monson and Mrs Turnure. Although only intimate friends and members of the two families had been invited, the religious ceremony and lunch held afterwards at the British Embassy by Sir Edward and Lady Monson were both extremely interesting. Pink flowers and palms decorated the altar and entrance of the church, whilst the fully choral service added charm to the simple function. The bride, Mrs Turnure, who is the daughter of General and Mrs Stone of New York, and widow of the late Mr Lawrence Turnure, looked very handsome in white crepe-de-chine, as shown by the sketch. Beautiful white lace and Irish guipure was encrusted in undulating fashion round the skirt, headed by mousseline roses. A white tulle hat, garnished with white plumes completed an effective ensemble. Mrs Stone was distinguished in mauve mousseline encrusted with black lace pastilles and piped with black ribbon as is here sketched. Lady Monson mother of the bridegroom was elegantly attired with black lace over white silk.

'The Hon Irma Monson, sister of the bridegroom, was in a pretty écru mousseline toilette. A dalmatique of écru filet was a becoming garniture to the front of the robe giving a princess effect which an accompanying large picture hat showed to advantage.'

Here is another piece of fulsome and ungrammatical reporting, entitled the *Admixture of Laces*.

'One of our great Houses has been making a wedding gown that is simply perfect. A notable feature in it was that the graceful flowing skirt had flounces of Point d'Alençon laid over gauzed ones edged with Valenciennes, and heading both was a line of white blooms. The two laces appeared again in the bodice. A cape berthe of Alençon had the Valenciennes peeping beneath. Some of the most fashionable blouses are of a coarse make of cream lace with motifs of black dentelle (lace) let in and many of the decolletages have black lace over white, and vice versa, while guipure d'art is continually embroidered with Maltese and old point. We let one lace into another in the most reckless fashion, considering that apart they have no features in common, while years ago they would have been heirlooms. Black Valenciennes is greatly asserting itself, and much of it has been painted, for painted lace is having a great following. Chiffon flowers in bold relief is being appliquéd on to a great many of the lace design in which two kinds appear.'

The Queen, one of the best known women's magazines, which described itself as a 'Ladies' Newspaper & Court Chronicle', featured a weekly column called 'Americans in London'. This covered the doings of all the important American men and women who appear to have formed a very large part of London society at this period. The column generally included the photograph of a titled lady of the English aristocracy who before her marriage had

Mrs Turnure's wedding dress. This white crêpe-de-chine and lace wedding dress was worn by Mrs Turnure, an American widow, at her marriage to Lord Monson in Paris. Drawing by P. Stevenson

Far left, above: **The Duke of York and Princess May of Teck, later George V and Queen Mary, on their wedding day surrounded by the bridesmaids.**/*Radio Times Hulton Picture Library*

Far left, below: **The indispensable teagown, circa 1893. It is in soft wool, shaded from creamy white to dark chestnut. The lightest tint is on the bodice, the deepest reaches to the edge of the triangular train. The sleeves have ruchings of white batiste with bands of guipure lace.**

belonged to an influential and wealthy American family. Accompanying copy would describe how and where she and her husband met, their respective family histories, who he was before he succeeded to the British title, where they lived, and how many children they had.

One such account describes the arrival of Mr Waldorf Astor in London for his daughter Pauline's wedding to Captain Spencer Clay. The following week the country was regaled with every detail of the wedding, the reception at Carlton House Terrace, the departure of the couple to Cliveden (Mr Waldorf Astor's country house) for the first part of their honeymoon, and the fact that Queen Alexandra gave the bride a golden cup, together with details of the costly jewels the bride's father had given her.

Through these columns one discovers that the Duchess of Roxburghe was formerly an American heiress, a Miss Mary Goelet; that the Countess of Essex was a Miss Adela Beach Grant of New York; that the Duchess of Manchester, a Miss Helena Zimmerman; and the Lady Yarmouth a Miss Thaw of Pittsburgh. One also finds, of course, the name of the famous Consuelo Vanderbilt, who married the Duke of Marlborough under such pressure from her mother — she afterwards maintained — that she was able to obtain an annulment of her marriage despite the fact that she had had children (she subsequently married a Frenchman, M. Jacques Balsan). We are also told that Cora, Lady Stafford, was the beautiful Mrs Colgate of New York who was 'early left a widow with an *immense* fortune and one daughter'! There was also the Marchioness of Dufferin and Ava, the Countess of Orford, the Countess of Donoughmore, and Lady Newborough — all Americans by birth.

Princess Alexis Dolgorouki née Miss Fleetwood Wilson./*The Lady's Realm*

What happened to all the English girls? Whom did *they* marry? The subject must have been much discussed, as a popular artist of the day, Harry Furniss, did a series of amusing full-page caricatures on this theme contrasting the American girl and her English counterpart (everything including drawings in this short period seems to have been on an extremely large scale).

The Lady's Realm of February 1903 attempts to answer this question in an article entitled 'English Wives of Foreign Noblemen' from which we learn that they may be divided into two categories. Those, who after marriage, continued to live chiefly in England, and those who not only adopted their husband's country but became practically foreigners themselves.

To the first class belonged Princess Victor Duleep Singh, née Lady Anne Coventry, Princess Alexis Dolgorouki née Miss Fleetwood Wilson, Baroness Eckhardstein née Miss Bundell Maple, Princess Henry of Pless née Miss Cornwallis West.

These are only a few of the heiresses mentioned and photographed in this article which also includes lengthy descriptions of such ladies as Lady Mary Hamilton who, having been unhappily married to a Prince of Monaco, afterwards became Countess Tassilo Festetics and spent all her life on her husband's Hungarian estates where 'King Edward, when Prince of Wales was entertained on more than one occasion.'

Lady Dorothy Walpole, having spent her childhood in Italy, where her somewhat eccentric mother, Lady Orford, gave parties in Florence which never started before midnight, married the Duc del Balzo and spent most of her life in Naples, where her entertaining was of a more serious order, her guests being cardinals, monsignori and clerics generally. A long list of titled Italian ladies follows, all of English birth, so one concludes that there were a number of wealthy British heiresses only too ready to exchange moneybags for exotic foreign titles and the warmth and less restricted atmosphere of southern Europe. There seemed to be no concealment of the fact that money was exchanged for titles, as at the head of the article is a drawing of a smiling young lady with a heart beneath her feet, holding a fat bulging moneybag in one hand and a coronet in the other!

It is obvious that women in this era had far more freedom. They are shown dining out in restaurants — unheard of in the previous century — walking on Scottish moors, bicycling, playing hockey and tennis, at the seaside in strange corsetted bathing dresses, and even driving an occasional car.

In the early 1900s the prevailing form of corset seems to have distorted the female figure even more than any of the earlier ones — and that is saying a great deal. The bust was made to look extraordinarily large and to stand out like a shelf in front, while the buttocks were pushed out behind into a large and very prominent rotunda. The stomach was completely flattened. With some truth the whole silhouette could be described as pornographic. The dresses swirled out with immense quantities of lace and embroidery insets, frills, bows, and fur and feather trimmings. As the vogue was for big puffed out hair-dos, transformations, wigs and postiches of all sorts were very necessary because the fashion was to wave the hair with curling tongs, in the process singeing and burning it so that it tended to fall out. False puffs were also used to build up the effect, and on these, secured by elaborate and frightening pins, were poised enormous Gainsborough hats which in their turn were decorated by buckles, feathers, bows, or whole birds, and flower gardens.

In addition to all these torments, among which one must not forget to mention extremely narrow pointed shoes, an arduous social discipline pronounced that clothes must be changed for each separate part of the social round. At weekend houseparties, so much enjoyed by King Edward, special changes of clothes were needed for church, for luncheon, for tea (tea gowns of great elaboration were now in fashion), for dinner and, of course, for all the sporting activities undertaken during the weekened. When not dressing and undressing, our Edwardian forbears ate enormous and complicated meals, not counting snacks on retiring which consisted of a variety of carefully covered sandwiches, biscuits in a labelled tin and an assortment of drinks on the bedside table. Naturally too, the arduous day could not start without tea and biscuits in bed.

It was a short but crowded epoch, the end of an era, summed up perhaps in the character of Edward VII, who in spite of his racy character, his cosmopolitan friends and love of all the good things of life, was a stickler for punctuality and etiquette.

Etiquette is also dealt with in the various magazine columns and the following extract obviously answers the worried questions of a widow contemplating remarriage. It is headed:

Etiquette

'1. Either of the colours you mention are appropriate. White also is permissible and is worn by young widows not as bridal attire but as a widow would wear a dress of grey or cream. Coloured embroidery is introduced when white is chosen to denote that it is not bridal white. 2. Yes, a hat or flower toque is usually worn. 3. Yes, she may carry a bouquet but *not* of white flowers only. 4. She should not have bridesmaids, but she may have pages. 5. Yes, she should have a wedding cake at the reception tea. 6. Wedding favours should *not* be given. 7. A relative should give the bride away, the bridegroom should be supported by a best man. 8. If not residing with her parents the invitations to the wedding should be issued in her name.'

The trousseaux were as complex and enormous as everything else in this era. It was now possible to produce quantities of all types of lace trimming and embroidery by machine. Thanks to the completely different attitude at court, parts of these frills and furbelows, such as elaborate petticoats, lacy camisoles, and embroidered stockings and the deep frills of lacy knickers, were allowed to be seen. Nightdresses, petticoats, knickers, chemises, stockings and pocket-handkerchiefs were all ordered in dozens and even by the gross and to these were added corsets, dressing jackets and teagowns. In the case of the nobility all of these garments were probably embroidered with coronets.

Teagowns had been widely used in the latter part of the 19th century, but were of a heavier type than the Edwardian silk and lace affair which gave its wearer such a fragile and diaphanous appearance at five o'clock tea.

A teagown from Liberty's is described in almost religious terms in 1904 as follows:

'It is frequently accounted to us for discredit that we are a nation devoid of all colour sense. But surely much may be forgiven us in that the house of Liberty discovered itself in England. Fashions may come and fashions may go but nothing disturbs the artistic balance of this wonderful establishment.

'The critical faculty departs from us as we enter into the suite of salons prepared, with a ready paean of praise, and a subsidiary prayer that we may not unduly be led into extravagance. Though pardon, forsooth, would be granted any woman who succumbed without resistance before that poem of a teagown (see page 64). Studiously severe in outline, with something a little puritan in its large flat collar, and cuffs of white Liberty satin embroidered with a pale green silk line, picked out with tiny crystals and gilt beads and larger green jewels. This is one of Liberty's strangely delicate green Nitas silks. The front opening upon a petticoat of soft white satin, the fulness whereof is caught to the figure by a jewelled belt.'

In 1910 *Les Modes* showed an enormous and very beautiful trousseau made for Princess Bonaparte. The numerous dresses were displayed on stands and the lingerie carefully arranged in dozens and all folded in the same way on a huge lace-covered table. Everything was hand embroidered, lace-edged, and threaded with ribbon. It was shown in a special building, the Hotel des Modes. Apparently the bride herself afterwards became the first woman psychoanalyst in France.

Towards 1905 a different fashion line was making its appearance. The corset had straightened out and the waistline was creeping upwards towards the bust. Several wedding dresses showed this new style. Dresses had a gradually increasing tendency to return to the lines of a hundred years before, while by 1910 the skirt line had become more and more constricted around the knees and the 'harem' style was in vogue. This line was obtained by various types of draping and swathing around the knee, by tunics worn one over the other and even by tying the legs together so that only tiny steps could be taken.

In spite of these self-inflicted restrictions, however, the papers were full of the doings of the suffragettes. Pictures showed them being forcibly fed, extricated from railings to which they had padlocked themselves, and carried off struggling to the cells by policemen. The writer herself knew one who had heaved a brick through one of the glass houses at Kew, while another was killed by throwing herself in front of the King's racehorse. The suffragette movement had been gradually growing in intensity since the eighties, but not only had it been opposed by Mr Gladstone, but also by Queen Victoria. Indeed, a large number of women did not approve of feminine emancipation. It was to take the experience and lessons of the First World War finally to get women the vote.

Princess Victor Duleep Singh, née Lady Anne Coventry./*The Lady's Realm*

Between 1910, when Edward VII died, and the outbreak of World War I in 1914, the pace of life began to quicken. Anarchy, revolution and change were in the air. Almost daily new technical processes were being invented and new machines were producing modern inventions on factory assembly lines.

French and English fashion periodicals of the period show us an enormous range of styles and a quite different variety of colours from those beloved by the Edwardians. The pale pinks and blues, lavenders, greys and blacks have been replaced by oranges, cerise, deep blues and violets, acid yellows and brilliant greens.

Some of these Eastern effects were partly due to the influence of the Diaghilev Russian Ballet, whose repertoire largely derived from oriental sources. At a time when the cinema was in its infancy and television was unknown, the theatre exerted an influence upon fashionable taste which should never be underestimated. The ballet *Scheherezade*, for example, produced in 1910 with scenery and costumes by Leon Bakst and music by Rimsky-Korsakov, depicting the violent but exciting 'goings-on' in the harem of a sultan while he was away, had a dynamic effect on the audience. After the first shock, Parisian society rushed out all agog to dress themselves and furnish their apartments and houses to resemble as nearly as possible the costumes and sets they had seen on the stage.

Below: **Bride in lace, circa 1919.** */Berthe Hemance*

Paul Poiret, the most famous French dress designer of the period, was just the man to help them. He himself loved foreign travel and understood the value of visiting museums for inspiration. During a visit to London he saw a Persian Exhibition of beautiful textiles and turbans at the Victoria and Albert Museum. He returned hot-foot to Paris to design for his customers exotic Eastern clothing based on the designs he had seen, and dressed his very elegant wife in oriental styles, complete with turban, feathers, jewels, tassels, brocades and oriental embroidery. He also gave a never-to-be-forgotten ball called 'The Thousand and Second Night' in which he appeared surrounded by slaves and to which Parisian society flocked, adorned in Eastern dress designed, of course, by Poiret.

The oriental influence was not confined to costume. In their homes people went in for black carpets, low divans, and Turkish tables. Cushions of all shapes and sizes in brilliant colours were strewn on the divans and on the floors. Incense smoke poured out of the mouths of Chinese idols. An illustration in a contemporary magazine sets the scene. A plain black-edged mirror is surmounted by a fan of highly coloured parrot feathers; two candles in holders are fixed on either side of the mirror, while below hang chains of beads, each loop ending in a tassel. The floor of the room is of royal blue felt, on top of which is an oval of black carpet. The curtains and cushions are of various blues and violets with touches of acid yellow. The electric light — a recent innovation — was concealed by a shade in the shape of a mandarin. Many a young bride of the period would set her heart on this type of interior decoration.

When the Russian Ballet opened in London in 1912 the effect was just as overwhelming as it had been in France. Later an American tour made just as much impact. After that one could not only dress like a Persian or Turkish slave, but also evoke in one's interior decoration the markets of North Africa and Spain. One could look Chinese or Japanese, ancient Greek, or 18th century, even early 19th century French peasant costumes from Eastern Europe were also copied, as were various Russian themes. The Russian Ballet repertoire at one time or another carried most of these themes in its decor and in costumes by some of the most famous artists of the period, such as Bakst, Benois, Picasso, Sert.

During World War I there was only a partial eclipse of fashion. The 1914-18 war had nothing like the same impact on the civilian population as Hitler's war and throughout it and for a few years after oriental themes remained popular. However, women were in tremendous demand, not only as nurses and secretaries, but as tram and lorry drivers, land girls and munition workers during the war; these activities demanded, on duty at least, that clothes were practical rather than frivolous.

Such a practical outfit might comprise a shapeless coat, a skirt cut level and reaching to just above the ankle with a normal waist-line worn with a hat of reasonable size. For the first time clerks appeared for work in blouses, coats and skirts, while a host of voluntary bodies joined by both men and women invented their own uniforms or semi-uniforms, which, with slight modifications both sexes wore.

A family photograph of the day shows the bridegroom in the uniform of the VAD (the Voluntary Aid Detachment). His bride, a beautiful auburn-headed girl with brown eyes, is in a brown coat and skirt falling just above the ankle, pale brown straw hat with roses, and brown suede shoes. These last were something very new. Under the coat is a charming diaphanous blouse of chiffon showing a lace-trimmed camisole threaded with ribbon.

Another group shows all the men in officer's uniform and the bride and bridesmaids in simple silk and chiffon and tulle dresses and veils. The bridesmaids' dresses have wide bands of ribbon decorating the tulle overskirts. One small bridesmaid is dressed in a pink voile dress copied from a Kate Greenaway picture with frills around the neck, sleeves and hem, a narrow black velvet band around the waist and a lacey Florentine straw bonnet tied with black velvet ribbon. She is wearing mittens and carries a basket of flowers. The wedding was in 1918 and the bride wore a dress ending some three or four inches above the ankle and a hem turned in to give it a harem line. White heather is mixed in her orange blossom

wreath. A line of small roses made of ribbon decorates the low square neckline of her gown and replicas of these tiny roses are also used on narrow bandeaus to keep the bridesmaids' veils in place.

In 1919 *Vogue* reported from Paris on Bridal Coiffures:

'The little French "peace-bride" is the fairest blossom of the spring. For Pierre and Jacques have come back from the front, the rank of captain resting with dignity on their twenty years, and they are claiming the young girls whom they left mere children. These youths show a new spirit; they look upon life with brave eyes, because they have known the life of war. Is it any wonder that we dare entrust to them our precious daughters? No, of a certainty, and that is why brides of recent months have been married in all their youthful grace almost childishly gauche, but always as exquisite as flowers just opening their petals in the early morning.

'The bridal gown of today is neither heavy, nor too rich nor too much trimmed. It must have an air of simplicity to match the simple charm of these young girls'.

Simple though they may have seemed, many of these same young girls in both England and France had been engaged in all sorts of war work, frequently on next to no food. The post-war woman for all her grace was no longer the pre-war shrinking violet.

When the war ended all those lucky enough to have survived the holocaust made haste to get married; and as women far outnumbered men there was a plentiful choice of brides. Trousseaux, of course, were much smaller and were no longer expected to last a lifetime as formerly — for one thing the postwar economic situation meant money was tight and for another, marriage had less permanence. As war weddings were notoriously hasty, quite a lot of them ended in divorce; and divorce itself was beginning to lose a great deal of its pre-war social stigma. Fashions too were more ephemeral. The corset had completely changed the prewar wineglass figure. The objective of fashionable young women was to be as flat back and front as possible. The bust was disappearing fast and so were those overemphasised buttocks and large hips. Slimming was the order of the day, both by diet and exercise and also by binders and bodices to flatten too exuberant female protrusions. Teenage girls frequently wore pieces of lace joined at the back by wide elastic, which effectually prevented them from ever developing a bust line.

The fashionable way to stand was to curve one's back and hollow the chest, poking the head forward — the very reverse of the stance of 'the fine woman' beloved of the Edwardians. Hair was getting shorter and a number of ardent fashion followers had theirs bobbed, though an equal number seem to have styled their hair in such a way that it only appeared short.

In the early 1920s women were still wearing evening dresses with trailing draperies, oriental brocades and embroideries. A favourite dance was the tango, then recently imported from South America, with its exciting Spanish-style rhythm. The complicated footwork and dashing poses of the dance lent themselves to full display of dresses with small trains or hanging panels.

Monkey fur was still being used on evening cloaks and also for daytime wear. By 1925 hemlines were gradually rising and the waist was getting lower. Hair was not only bobbed, but shingled, bingled and 'eton-cropped'. Women had finally got the vote in 1920; the war had proved without doubt the debt the country owed them and though they were still decades away from getting equal pay for equal work, the historic imbalance between men and women was beginning to be righted. Perhaps the very masculinity of the fashions of the day was a measure of the readjustment.

Changes of taste produced some casualties, however, and Poiret who had been unable to adapt his outlook on fashion to modern trends, fell from being King of Fashion in the prewar era to die in poverty in the 1920s. Diaghilev, on the other hand, was always looking into the future. He continued to employ modern designers, including rising Cubist artists like Picasso, Braque, Gontcharova and Larionov, until his death in 1929.

Cubist art was to prove the inspiration of late twenties fashion. One has only to look at the inherently geometrical shapes formed by straight-seamed garments hung on a completely flattened figure, topped by a headhugging cloche hat, to realise what Cubism was all about.

The fashionable designer, Chanel, a young emancipated French woman, was most sympathetic to the new feeling. The skirt was at its shortest in 1927 and the waist at its lowest, and for the new 'boyish' girl Chanel designed her famous jumper and cardigan suits, using completely new materials and in greys, browns and navy blues. Her evening dresses, however,

Left: **Part of a trousseau, circa 1927; note the hair style, shoes and short skirt.**

were more feminine, featuring filmy pleated silks and laces. Perhaps she had in mind that the Frenchwoman's shorter and rather more thickset figure did not look so well in the boyish styles as did the taller and more angular English or American woman. Chanel's bridal dresses were also feminine and at the same time simple in line. Some of them were very short with long trains from the shoulder — a rather odd combination, especially when there was often a long veil as well.

The short skirt provoked intense anger and even legislation in the more backward parts of America. States like Utah and Ohio were particularly outraged. But the whole social ethos was changing. Registry office weddings were more common and birth control became a subject for discussion, at least in private, as Dr Marie Stopes through her books and lectures began her life-long campaign for sex education and enlightenment.

About this time a very unusual wedding took place in the south of England. The setting was a cathedral and the bride was dressed entirely in silver, the dress being long-waisted and full-skirted, reaching to just above the ankles. The sleeves were long and tight and a long veil, falling over the face, completely covered the dress. The veil was held in place by a deep circlet of orange blossom. The six bridesmaids were all dressed in gold dresses of a similar style and carried sprigs of orange tree bearing small oranges and bound with silver ribbon. The bride bore a sheaf of white and gold lilies. The feminine woman was on her way back.

In the early thirties bridal dresses were simple and well cut, but they were often spoilt, as in this case, by heavy bouquets. Drawing by P. Stevenson

This trend became more apparent from 1930 onwards. The ideal feminine form was reminiscent of the classical Greek statue — tall and well-proportioned, with a flat back, a slightly indented waist, small round breasts and long, slender legs. Madeleine Vionnet, a French designer famous for her cross or bias cutting of material, made these classical styles supremely attractive. She, and later Christian Dior, were the two French designers who could best be described as architects in material. The classical style needs length and a number of stylistic devices were introduced to give short skirts that illusion. Some were long at the back, others had long floating side panels; others still were cut in tiers, longer behind than before. Then there was the transparent overskirt with a shorter underskirt. The skirt also varied in length according to the time of day and the occasion. A white wedding dress or an evening dress, for example, would be floor length and an afternoon dress about 12in from the ground, but a morning dress 13-14in above the ground. The majority of women were busy by day, either running a household without help or doing a job outside the home. In the evening there was time for more formal dress.

All the white wedding dresses of this period show the same type of simple well-cut refined design: a short or closely arranged hair-style, and a smallish wreath or coronet with a veil generally attached at the back. This created an effect of height and grace, the head appearing small in proportion to the body. Underneath, a corselet which combined a bra and corset all in one produced the required sheathlike elegance, in which no part of the torso was emphasised. Tall girls were in fashion — and those not so endowed strove to achieve at least the impression of willowy height. Popular bouquets were sheafs which appeared to lie along the arm, but in some cases the effect was overdone: the bride had her work cut out to hump her bouquet down the aisle and unlucky was the weakling bridesmaid who caught it!

The woman who probably most personified the ideal of this period was Greta Garbo. Unlike many other film idols she survived the transition from the silent films to the 'talkies'. In such parts as Ninotchka, Queen Christina, and Karin in *Two-Faced Woman*, she typified the tall, slim, emancipated yet thoroughly feminine woman. Films and filmstars like Garbo were, in fact, as much an influence on clothes in the 1930s as the theatre had been in the previous century. In some old cinemas it it still possible to come across versions of that strange, supposedly 'Cubist' architecture which influenced many young brides in their choice of a home, especially when the films they saw on the screen were set in a world of 'cubist' furniture, where glass, chrome and marble made up the ideal 'love nest', with its uncomfortable and impossibly heavy 'cubist' three-piece suites.

The most popular Royal wedding of the early 1930s was that of Princess Marina of Greece to the Duke of Kent, the youngest of the Royal dukes. She was married in Westminster Abbey in 1934. Her wedding gown was a long, beautifully cut design of white and silver brocade, with an English rose motif. It had a very long train and a veil attached to the back of a tiara. (This same diamond tiara incidentally was worn by Princess Marina's daughter, Princess Alexandra, at her wedding in 1963). The bridal bouquet was a sheaf of lilies and there were eight bridesmaids of whom two were children — our present Queen being one, and Lady Mary Cambridge the other. All the wedding clothes were designed by Molyneux.

The royal bride had been living in Paris and travelled to England by boat and train, arriving in a pink-beige crêpe cloqué dress and a three-quarter length coat trimmed with fox, a beige hat with beige and brown ostrich feathers drooping over the brim on one side. Beige, of course, was a new and very fashionable colour at this time. The Princess was also responsible for creating a highly popular colour of her own — a shade of turquoise which quickly became known as 'Marina' blue.

Princess Marina's trousseau aroused a great deal of interest, as it was obvious from the first that she had a sense of style and fashion until then rare among royal ladies. The *Illustrated London News* devoted two pages to drawings and descriptions of its most important coats, dresses and accessories.

To quote: 'Her eye, that of a trained artist, appreciates the beauty of simple unbroken lines and her originality of outlook is reflected in her choice of accessories and details'. Among examples illustrated by sketches were a high-necked evening dress of black cloqué satin, the skirt slit to reveal a stripe of silver lamé; the sash was of lamé lined with petunia crêpe. A belt and gloves of natural pigskin lined with black velvet looked most intriguing in conjunction with a wide-shouldered black-velvet gown. Another evening ensemble was of *bois-de-rose faconné*, with a loose coat of beige velvet lined to match the dress. An afternoon ensemble was in heavy crinkly crêpe with a coat trimmed with dyed fox. Other items were: a black box calf leather belt marking the waist of a black woollen coat with a draped collar of astrakhan; an almond green morning outfit trimmed with nutria; and a black crêpe afternoon frock; its loose sleeves and hem edged with a self fringe and round its neck a tie of orange velvet.

When the engagement was announced the couple were staying in Yugoslavia and the peasants gathered to congratulate them and present them with bouquets. The princess was also given a crown of red flowers, the same flowers forming the bouquet presented to the prospective bridegroom. Her bouquet was of red rowan berries, blue gentians and white edelweiss.

The wedding in Westminster Abbey, was preceded by an elaborate and beautiful Orthodox church ceremony, as the bride's father was Greek and her mother Russian. The two small bridesmaids attended with lighted tapers and the bridal crowns were exchanged and held over the couple's heads according to custom.

Messrs McVitie & Price, the biscuit makers, created an extravaganza of a wedding cake — a brilliant and delicate sugar edifice, eight feet high, surrounded by white heather, roses, and lilies of the valley. Concealed in the first wedge to be cut at the wedding breakfast were seven charms of solid gold representing a wedding ring, a thimble, a bachelor's button, a horseshoe, a dove, a donkey, and a threepenny bit!

The newspapers and magazines described the interior of the royal couple's new home, 3 Belgrave Square, and the various rooms were photographed, so that the public at large could appreciate the elegance and artistry which had been devoted to the decoration. The beautiful presents of jewels and works of art which had been specially chosen for the royal couple because of their appreciation and knowledge of the arts were also photographed and described in great detail. The magazine *Vogue* devoted a special number entirely to the wedding. It made a particular feature of a portrait in colour by Erickson of the Princess in a pink and red dress with unusual sleeves and two large chrysanthemums, one pink and one red on the corsage.

In 1935, the enterprising but then unknown dress designer, Norman Hartnell, sent a number of sketches to Lady Alice Montague-Douglas-Scott before her marriage to the Duke of Gloucester and was forthwith commissioned to design the bridal outfit for the wedding. He became renowned throughout the world for the clothes he designed for royal occasions and also for the magnificent embroideries with which most of them were covered.

Another pre-war 'royal' wedding which attracted great public interest was that in 1937 of the sparkling and witty American, Mrs Wally Simpson to the Duke of Windsor, after the world-shattering events of the Abdication. The gown was created by Mainbocher, an American designer, and is described by Cecil Beaton in his diary as being of a 'hard shade of blue'. It was very slim-fitting with long sleeves, and decorated in front by a row of tiny buttons. Her hat was decorated with matching blue feathers and a halo of blue tulle.

The 1920s also saw increasingly widespread use of what we now call 'synthetic fibres'. The first of these was artificial silk, which was used in particular for stockings and lingerie. It was also developed into all sorts of fabrics for use in dresses, particularly of the crêpe variety. Thus cheap, attractive but silky-textured garments for the first time came within the buying capacity of most women. True these fabrics had their disadvantages; they were difficult to wash and iron as they had a habit of shrinking into nothing suddenly if damped, and a too-hot iron would cause them to shrivel up. These hazards apart, however, artificial silk meant silk-clad legs for many and flimsy underclothes trimmed with lace in every trousseau.

Towards the end of the 1930s, under the shadow of approaching war, women's clothes took on a romantic quality. Fashion was built around the upswept hairstyle which was something of a bombshell in 1938. This immediately gave a late Victorian appearance to the female head and, in keeping, waists became tight and shoulders, already square, went up in the manner of the 1890s. Strangely-shaped hats, poised at extraordinary angles, appeared to alight on the head. Almost any type of skirt was acceptable, but particularly popular was the Austrian dirndl — a skirt of varying length, fully gathered at the waist.

In Paris, Schiaparelli with her cosmopolitan outlook on colours, shapes and accessories, gave fashion a surrealistic touch. Surrealism was the important art movement of the time and Salvador Dali, its most famous exponent.

All shades of violet and mauve were popular and attempts were made to revive the crinoline.

A dress by the French designer Vionnet made in 1926 but very typical of the thirties. It was of crêpe satin and shows the bias cut for which Vionnet became famous. Drawing by P. Stevenson

Right: **Ready for church, circa 1940.**/*Barnaby's Picture Library*

On the other hand there was increasing interest in trousers and turbans, a rig-out which was to be the most popular and practical war-time dress of the next five years.

An American edition of *Vogue* for October 1938 contains illustrations of two sumptuous wedding dresses; one, long-sleeved in Ottoman silk, small-waisted and full-skirted by Balenciaga; the other of oriental magnificence, a silver sheath by Molyneux. The latter is described as 'sultanic' because of the enormously wide necklace of pearls and brilliants filling in the low round neckline. The bride in the illustration also wears a chaplet of pearls dipping over her forehead in true Indian fashion. The dress has leg o'mutton sleeves — thought to make the throat look delicate.

A dirndl wedding dress, one of the season's most popular styles, could be had in white satin, taffeta or bengaline. The bride was adjured by *Vogue* to have her bridesmaids dressed in velveteen dirndls, which would look really 'Old World', and to have them in all shades of violet! Nosegays of violets were popular for the wedding bouquet and in fact violets and various shades of mauve were described in almost poetically lyrical terms. Another fancy of the time was circular bunches of gladioli, all stripped off their stems, poor things!

For a wedding in a house (the type often seen in American films of the period) Mainbocher designed a violet moiré dress with violets on the shoulders and violet clusters clipped to the ears; it was worn with long violet gloves. Muffs of all sorts were in vogue and a bride dressed by Schiaparelli in a cameo-pink jacket with shirred-doll waist and framing skunk collar was ordered 'not to miss her chance of carrying a skunk muff'! This outfit was described as ideal for the bride who wanted to look glamorous in City Hall, but at the same time wanted to avoid fuss and bother.

One of Chanel's outfits in Parma violet was accompanied by a violet velvet hat with a flighty pink feather attached. About this, however, brides were cautioned to find out first whether their husbands-to-be would object!

The war ended all such frivolity and fashion magazines from 1940 onwards gradually diminished in size as paper became increasingly scarce. Such articles and advertisements as did appear were all geared to coping with shortages. Make-do-and-mend, clothes rationing, and what to do between air raid warnings and on the long dark evenings during the blackout, were the main topics.

In one magazine of 1943 the only reference to a bridal outfit appeared above an advert urging readers to have their old corsets remade 'as new' for 12s 6d. A small drawing showed a short skimpy woollen dress with a short jacket, with three rows of some simple decorative outlining around the yoke on both dress and jacket. No hat or any other accessory was shown and readers were advised that the outfit 'would do for the wedding and long after'.

There were articles on how to knit and crochet and otherwise concoct your own hats. You could, for instance, obtain an old Serviceman's hat, cut away the peak and trim it with a band and pom-pom of fur from an old fur coat, making the piece that went round the armhole into a fur necktie. Very smart too!

Whole garments were picked apart, turned and remade with and without alteration, and this applied to coats as well as dresses. A type of bright, almost fluorescent yellow nylon used in supply parachutes was sometimes sold as war surplus material; this was eagerly bought to make briefs and panties — the panels were not big enough for anything else. Stockings were mostly of lisle or artificial silk. (Even as late as 1948 it was still impossible to buy nylon stockings in English shops.)

During the war itself nylons could sometimes be obtained surreptitiously on the black market or were brought in from abroad — they were a favourite 'sweetener' of American servicemen. Real silk stockings were hoarded for special occasions, like weddings. Happy was the bride whose husband had leave for the wedding and twice as happy if by hook or crook, by begging, borrowing or inheriting she could get a piece of fabric to make a wedding dress. The Hon Sarah Norton did just that in 1945 when she married the Hon W. W. Astor (RNVR) MP in a Jacqmar dress made from some brocaded satin inherited from her grandmother. She decorated it with a butterfly brooch made from unique stones her grandfather had collected — purple diamonds. Brocade was much in favour as it could be had in furnishing fabric, and used afterwards as an evening dress.

Frequently arrangements for the wedding had to be made by the bride herself as not only the bridegroom but the best man as well was on active duty. The location of Service units meant that quiet country churches were popular venues for wartime weddings but there could be no wedding bells of any sort; they were the warning of invasion. There were few choir boys or bridesmaids as a rule, for many children had been evacuated either to remote parts of the country or abroad, and often other potential attendants were either in the Forces, on the land, driving ambulances or buses, or making munitions.

The parents of the bride had possibly never seen their future son-in-law, so that important figure-head, the bride's mother, had very little to say in any of the arrangements. Sugar rationing meant that there could be little or no icing on the wedding cake, and various decorative tea-cosy effects were achieved to prettify it.

For those who could manage to obtain them, some of the famous stores advertised pearl-embroidered satin gowns with orange blossom, and several Mayfair firms made small trousseaux in such materials as artificial satin — and even found lace to trim them. A lady in the country specialised in the supply of bridal wreaths. To give the wartime bride a firm base, there were foundation garments but the amount of elastic used was rigorously controlled as was the type of material used and the fastenings. At one point in the war it was threatened that suspenders would disappear, to be replaced by buttons and loops, and all old metal fastenings had to be hoarded.

Many young brides were themselves in uniform, belonging to the ATS, the WRNS, the WAAF, and other uniformed organisations. They frequently got married in uniform and benefiting from the fact that many tailoring firms formerly specialising in high quality men's wear had been directed into military tailoring, the Service girls made attractive, even chic brides. A particularly smart item was the Service great coat and warm double-breasted ATS coats sold for £9.00 — a considerable price in those days.

The wartime Board of Trade commissioned a range of 'utility' clothes from various well-known designers of the time. In silhouette they showed a simple knee-length, slightly flared or pleated skirt, and square-shouldered top with a well-marked waist and very little trimming. Trousseaux were designed along these lines, and generally consisted of a coat and skirt, a long coat, a short dress and jacket and a long dress for evenings, with or without sleeves, according to the season. The inevitable slacks, blouses, and wool jumpers and cardigans completed the wardrobe of the wartime bride. Once married she might become the make-do-and-mend addict who reputedly wrote to the Board of Trade as follows:-

'My husband wanted some new shirts, so in order to save precious coupons, this is what happened. I undid a blue and white pin check cotton washing frock of my own, washed it carefully and it was made into a short-sleeved shirt, with four collars to match.

Out of an old sheet which was only worn in parts, I made two shirts with undetachable collars. Also out of remnants of other sheets I got six pairs of shorts (underpants) for him, using the elastic from the tops of his old ones. Also there was enough material to make six soft collars, a dozen handkerchiefs and several table napkins and pillowslips'.

She had an almost visible halo. Cotton, coming as it did from overseas, was very scarce and was also needed for munitions.

An invaluable service for brides in the austerity period after the war was started by Moss Bros. More and more women officers had been in the habit of getting their uniforms from Moss Bros during the latter part of the war, but while men had been able to hire suits and uniforms of all kinds since 1897, there was no such hiring service for women. In 1947 a WAAF officer wanting very much to have a white wedding, was bemoaning the fact that though she had the money she had not enough coupons for the purpose. One of the Moss Bros directors heard of her plight, bought a wedding dress from the firm's coupon reserve and hired it to her. It was the beginning of a new service and now, not only the bride's dress and those of the bridesmaids and pages, but even model hats for the bride's mother can all be hired, together with wreaths, veils, and tiaras.

The great occasion of 1947 was the marriage of our present Queen, then Princess Elizabeth, to Prince Philip of Greece, now Duke of Edinburgh.

The Princess's dress was designed by Norman Hartnell in ivory satin, embroidered on the skirt and bodice with roses, star flowers, and orange blossom in pearl and crystal, the inspiration coming from a Botticelli picture. With this she wore a diamond tiara and veil. The bodice had what was known as a 'sweetheart' neckline and the skirt flared out gently towards the hem. There were eight grown-up bridesmaids and two pages. The whole effect of the bridal procession was fairy-like and ethereal, as the embroidered stars and flowers appeared to float and glitter on the filmy material of the dresses. The bridesmaids' dresses were arranged with great delicacy, to preserve the impression of lightness and grace.

A family group shows the bride and bridegroom surrounded by royal relatives, some reigning monarchs, others who were living in exile, but all dominated by the matriarchal figure of Queen Mary in one of her famous toques. The chief bridesmaid was Princess Margaret, wearing a dress very similar in shape and material to the bride's, with long white gloves and a wreath of upstanding white flowers. The two little pages had white blouses, Scottish kilts and sporrans.

The decade which followed — the 1950s — saw the reappearance of romantic feminine styling with emphasis on the bust, waist and hips, full skirts or very tight figure hugging skirts and increasingly high heels, leading eventually to the highly impractical stiletto heel. Fashion models in contemporary photographs are shown poised on these ungainly pivots in various unlikely positions, archly looking sideways at the camera out of the

Two brides in 1951 showing the return to a Victorian 'prettiness', now that clothes were no longer rationed. Drawing by P. Stevenson

corners of their eyes, usually holding a bag and invariably gloved. Their carefully-shaped, very red mouths seem always to be smiling, on occasions even simpering, and their general coquettishness is heightened by firmly defined, hard make-up. The whole effect was regarded at the time as well-groomed, elegant, and ladylike — three words which were less emphasised in the fashions of the 1960s and have a dated ring among the trendy, casual younger generation of the 1970s.

Films, the great arbiters of taste in the 1950s, had the same romantic approach to behaviour and fashion. Women, one might have been led to believe, were obsessed with the idea of catching themselves a man and getting married to him at all costs. In a way this attitude was strongly reminiscent of the Victorians, but it is by no means uncommon in the aftermath of major wars when a generation of eligible males has been decimated by casualties. The effect after World War II was not so marked as after World War I, but no young woman in the 1950s wished to risk being left on the shelf like so many of her maiden aunts. It was hardly surprising that the female sex symbol — Marilyn Monroe and her like — was so revered.

In France, Christian Dior was the king of fashion. After he had successfully launched his calf-length 'New Look' in 1947, he followed it with various fashion 'lines' which were awaited with breathless interest every spring and autumn until his untimely death in 1954. We had the H line, an inverted Y line in 1955, also a 'tulip' and a 'scissor' line; none of them, however, achieved the widespread popularity of the New Look. Dior's designs all stood out from the work of other designers, however, by virtue of their architectural quality. They had an immense influence on fashion.

With the ending of post-war shortages there was time to experiment with and produce all types of man-made fibres. Such names as Orlon, Dacron, Tricel, Acrilan, and Terylene all common now, but then very new, appeared on advertisement pages. All types of clothes, from night to day wear and for all seasons, were made from these fabrics, and a bride could have her whole wedding outfit — dress, veil, shoes, stockings and gloves and most of her trousseau — made from synthetic fabrics. Transparent and semi-transparent nighties were popular and could be had in all colours and decorated with nylon lace. The trousseau would last for years if care was taken never to subject the garments to too much heat. The main drawbacks were that whites yellowed with age and washing and the early type of nylon, being non-porous, was uncomfortable to wear in hot weather despite its lightness and silky finish. In winter, however, a bride could go on her honeymoon in a very expensive-looking but simulated 'fur' coat and carry an artificial leather hand-bag that was indistinguishable from the real thing — and both at a fraction of the price.

In the 1960s there was a growing realisation, especially among the young, of the dangers and uncertainties of a world in which nuclear weapons existed in large numbers and in which capitalism and communism seemed to be heading inevitably towards another conflict. The inherent lack of security and balance led to a questioning of earlier standards and values. Nowhere was this reflected more conspicuously than in the way people chose to dress. Gone were the romantic and rather coy women of the 1950s. Not only young girls but young men paraded all kinds of wild and exciting clothes, strange hair-dos and even stranger make-up. Taken to extremes — as many trends were — this last became exceedingly complicated. It amounted to a modern form of mediaeval face-painting, in which the various colours were put on in layers by brushes and worked into each other, just as an artist paints a picture.

This radical change in fashion outlook was not very obvious till around 1966 when it erupted in a welter of all sorts of styles. There were no longer such words in fashion terms (as well as others) as 'must' or 'cannot'. One could be anything or look anyhow as long as one was young or looked it. Wigs, long hair, elaborate plaits of artificial hair or careful short cuts — all were possible. There were no established rules but emphasis on the bust, waist and hips declined and as skirts got ever shorter and jeans ever tighter it became obvious that the crotch was the centre of attention.

The mini skirt was possibly one of the ugliest fashions in history because it suited only a few well-proportioned slim girls, yet although they looked repellent or ridiculous, less endowed heavy-limbed women insisted on wearing it. Nonetheless the 1960s produced a new breed of young and previously unknown designers like Courrèges, Ungaro, Emmanuelle Khanh and Mary Quant who blossomed out almost overnight. To balance out the brevity of the miniskirt, boots of ever increasing length were worn winter and summer and frequently on what seemed the most unsuitable occasions and not just with mini-skirts, but teamed up with long flowing oriental dresses as well.

In 1968 and 1969 fashion models were pictured in 'space age' clothes designed in various plastics and vinyl materials, reflecting man's first landing on the moon. The plastic 'wet look' was promoted in the fashion magazines at the end of the decade but towards the 1970s it became clear that all types of clothing were possible as long as they expressed the wearer's individual opinions or emotions in conformity or otherwise to established ideas. Among the young, hair got longer and longer, and as the idea of being well-groomed was 'out', it was acceptable even when straggling and matted. There was a rush to street markets to get old fur coats and secondhand dresses and old patched jeans. These were worn with boots, large hats, and quantities of oriental

and secondhand jewellery of all types. Boys and girls frequently could not be distinguished except by their voices.

At the same time hemlines gradually descended after various set-backs and the older women were at last able to feel fashionable in a midi or knee-length skirt. Trouser suits were worn by all. While this was happening, footwear fashionable with the younger set was getting ever more solid and clumping, until by 1973 many girls appeared to be wearing surgical boots.

Brides reflected these strange extremes of fashion, particularly in artistic circles, the stage and high fashion. However, many brides still went to the altar in the conventional long white silk or satin dress with veil and bouquet, held a reception afterwards at which they cut their wedding cake, and glided off in a cloud of paper confetti to a sunny spot on the Mediterranean. However they may have dressed on other occasions, they felt extremes of fashion were out of place at a wedding. They also felt it right and proper to be married in a church, even though they never attended one at any other time in their life.

The post-war years have increasingly emphasised the importance of advertising. From it has stemmed a wide variety of aids to personal choice — for example, a whole range of services for the bride-to-be. We have *Vogue's Bride Book,* which covers all aspects of bridal fashion — make-up, hair styles, the dress, ring, bouquet, trousseau, veil or hat. The actual ceremony, presents, reception and honeymoon are discussed, too, as well as medical advice on birth control. Valuable advice is given on the buying and furnishing of the new home.

Many of the big stores have wedding present services, by means of which intending gift donors can choose a suitable gift from among a shelf of objects previously selected by the bride and groom. The gift is then dispatched by the store, properly wrapped with an attractive greeting card enclosed. This ensures that the happy couple really get what they want to furnish their new home.

Then, too, there are endless varieties of invitation cards suitable for every type of person. One firm makes a speciality of wedding stationary in matching colours and appropriate designs. These include the invitations, wedding cake cards, menu cards, table napkins, which all match. The Post Office provides special greeting telegrams for congratulations. We have already spoken of the various hiring services available, which have increased in number and range in the last 30 years. The travel agency trade offers special packaged honeymoon trips and certain hotels cater for honeymoon couples, with bridal suites set aside especially for their use.

By 1974 the mini skirt was definitely on the way out and the vogue for enormous soles and heels appeared to have passed its peak. Suddenly it seemed it was both fashionable and enjoyable to be well groomed again.

But what of love, marriage and wedding ceremonies? Well, despite women's liberation movements and all the upheavals in manners and morals of the past 14 years, all seem still to be with us. No one has been able to come up with a workable alternative to marriage which, with all its faults, gives a sense of security to the partners and, more important, to the children. Communes have been tried but do not last long; and the majority of people still hanker after romance. There was, for instance, just as much interest in Princess Anne's wedding in 1973 as there had been in Princess Alexandra's ten years before.

Although there were a number of unusual weddings in the late 1960s the bride of the mid-1970s seems to want to return to Victorian fragility and to look ultra-feminine. Delicate colours, veils, flowered hats and bonnets, and ethereal trailing dresses are the order of the day.

Strange are the ways of fashion, or should we say, woman? Why should the woman of today hanker for the illusion of Victorian bondage while at the same time seeking 'liberation'? Is this just a blind? Or is it a rebellion against the obsessive uglification of all aspects of life including fashion, in the immediately preceding years. Only time can unravel the paradox.

Left: **The Mini-skirted bride of 1968 in a dress of woven silk ribbons.**

Before 1800

Right: **A medieval woodcut showing the Bishop blessing the nuptial bed and sprinkling it with Holy Water.***/Mary Evans Picture Library*

Far right: **Marriage at the church porch. The two fathers-in-law hold the bride's train during the ceremony which is completed before the couple enter the church. The bride wears her hair loose as a sign of virginity. Circa 1460. Drawing by P. Stevenson.**

Below right: **The marriage of Henry VI to Margaret of Anjou. 15th century.***/Mary Evans Picture Library*

Left: **A rather untidy bride awaiting her husband in bed.**

Below left: **Betrothal of Joanna of Castile to the Archduke Philip.**

Right: **The bride being given good advice before being helped to undress and get into bed. 16th century.**

Below right: **A 16th century bride. John of Winchcomb, a famous clothier known as 'Jack of Newbury', married this young woman who was described as "habited in a gown of sheep's russet, and a kirtle of fine worsted, her head attired with a billiment of gold, and her hair as yellow as gold hanging down behind her which was curiously combed and plaited. She was led to church by two boys with bride laces and rosemary tied about their silken sleeves".**

Left: **A German Jewish bride after Boener with her mother and mother-in-law. The bride wears a marriage girdle while the two older women wear the Synagogue ruffs and cloaks. 1705.**

Below left: **Newlyweds praying, or first things first. 16th century.***/Mary Evans Picture Library*

Right: **First night trouble in the 18th century.**/*Mary Evans Picture Library*

Below: **A Catholic marriage in France, before the Revolution, circa 1739. The couple seem to be of noble birth, and the ceremony in a private chapel.**/*Mary Evans Picture Library*

A proposal of marriage

Madam,

When I see you, on your gravity and looks I conclude you to be a suitable wife for me. My first, when I saw her, told me she intended to marry; being weary of boarding, she would have a house and table of her own. If you should be sick, no one would be so tender to you as a husband. My last wife had seven hundred pounds ready cash. She brought me a silver tankard cost three pounds more, and twelve silver spoons, and as many suits of grave silks which cost above forty pounds, and were laced with gold and silver up to the pocket holes; the best of these I save for you.

My father gave me twelve hundred pounds besides my education. I have been a good husband and settled my family. My eldest son has a living about £120 per ann. a minster; my second son has two places and teaches school. They have been over two years on their own. My third son is married; he is a confectioner and grocer, selling tea, chocolate and coffee, which he roasts. He had £800 with his wife; and now eighty pounds a year has come to her by her brother's death. I have two daughters at home; the youngest as tall as yourself; they have their portions set out. My eldest son is to pay them out of my perpetual advowson, which is settled on him after my death. My eldest daughter has twice lived with her brother the confectioner, and intends to go again as soon as I marry. Then I have but one daughter who shall wait upon us, and my maid you shall choose. My brewing an old man servant does; and I hire a washerwoman; so that you and I may enjoy ourselves with all the exquisite pleasures of matrimony so long as God shall send us life and health.

I understand physick. My first wife died in childbed; my last wife would not take anything to stop her looseness, though I have cured many of it. The fever seized her vitals, she was sick for more than three days. I had four eminent doctors; but she would take nothing they presented: said she was burnt up, scorched within and their cordials were too hot for her.

Oh! Madam, fear nothing; a house I have well furnished, and no one to molest me. I have lived above 30 years in Apsley, and have above £150 per annum. I have only one grandchild. I beg an answer. Please, madam, to direct me.

Edw. Hill, Rector, Apsley, Nr Woburn.

Left: **A proposal of marriage in 1749.**

Below left: **The bridegroom in his nightcap about to join his bride in bed. Picart 1737.**/*Mary Evans Picture Library*

Far left: **The reluctant bride and the ardent bridegroom. J. B. Simonet and Moreau le jeune, after Baudouin.**/*Mary Evans Picture Library*

Left: **The wedding day. The two lines of verse beneath the picture cynically warn the bride to treasure every happy moment of this day as love will vanish as the novelty of the wedding wears off. J. B. Patas after Eisen. France circa 1760.** /*Mary Evans Picture Library*

Right: **A wax doll dressed as a bride and marked "Mrs Powells wedding suite 1761". The doll was possibly made and carefully dressed to show a customer how she would look in the finished gown.** */Victoria and Albert Museum*

Below: **An English silk tissue wedding dress, worn in 1782.***/Victoria and Albert Museum*

Left: **A white satin dress said to have been a wedding dress worn about 1780.** */Victoria and Albert Museum*

Below: **Fleet weddings were performed within the jurisdiction of the Fleet prison by discredited clergymen, often ex-prisoners, the ceremony taking place in an ale-house. All sorts of rackets developed — false certificates were given, ceremonies ante-dated, while young heiresses were decoyed into marrying villains or penniless adventurers. Such practices were finally ended in 1754 by act of Parliament, but there was much opposition to the act from all levels of society — people had become accustomed to the ease and speed with which marriages could be finalised if the need arose.***/Mary Evans Picture Library*

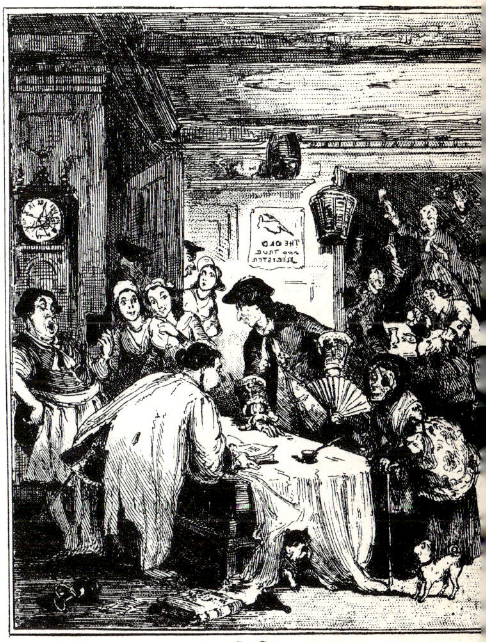

Fleet Marriages.

1800~1900

Right: **A bridal dress in white satin and embroidered net, and veil of Devon bobbin lace, worn in 1848.**/*Victoria and Albert Museum*

Far right, above: **The penny wedding.** /*Mary Evans Picture Library*

Far right, below: **The marriage contract, Paris, early 19th century.**/*Mary Evans Picture Library*

Matchmaking. From a painting by H. Helmick. */Mary Evans Picture Library*

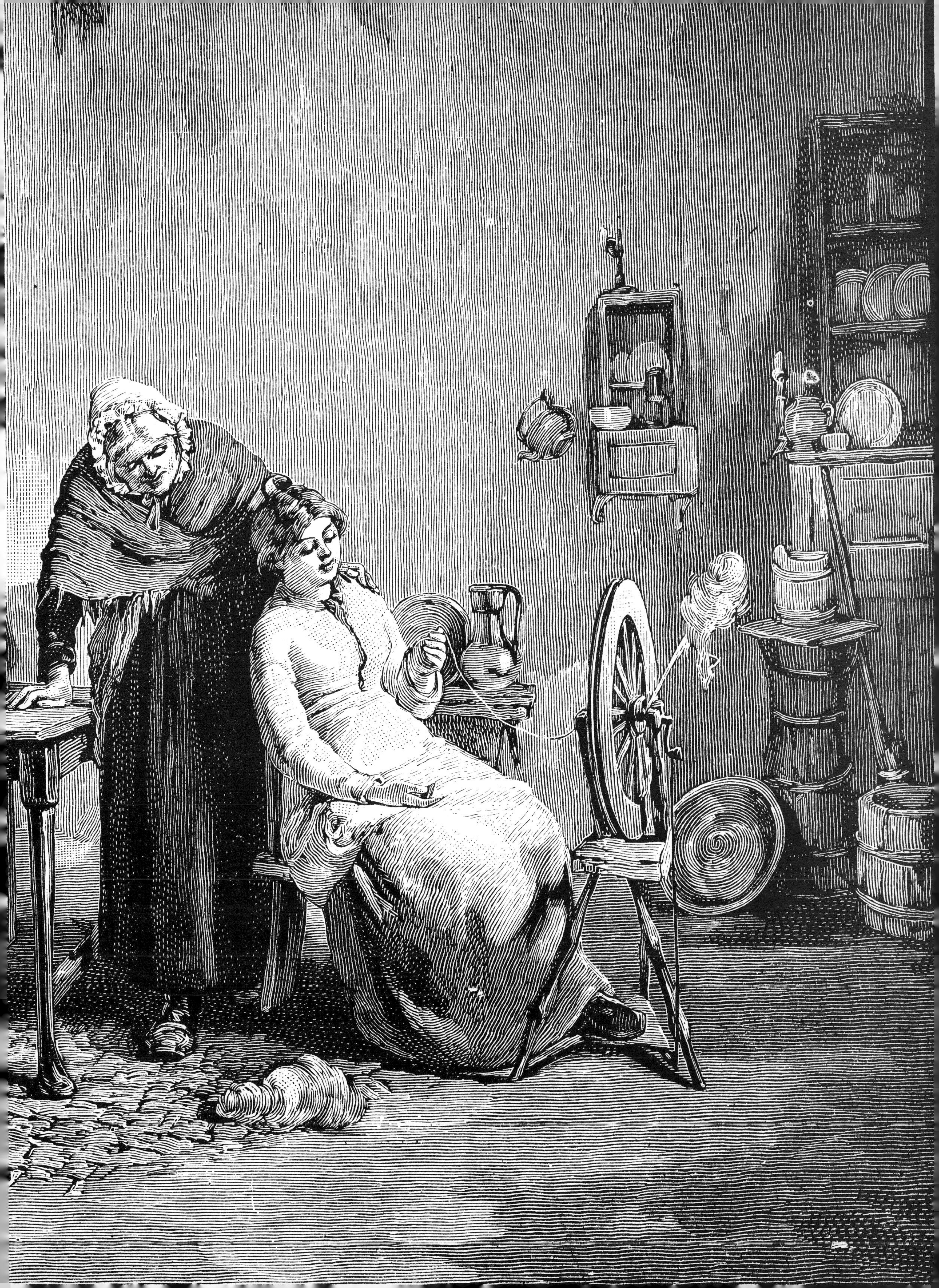

The Matrimonial Arrangement Association (Limited.)

 "The Happiest moment of my life ——"

Far left, above: **The Matrimonial Arrangement Assocation Limited, 1867.** */Punch*

Far left, below: **The happiest moment of my life. G. C. Cruikshank from the** *Comic Almanack 1850./Mary Evans Picture Library*

Far left: **A wedding dress of cotton embroidery on muslin worn in October 1848 by Mrs M. H. Woolmer./***Victoria and Albert Museum*

Left: **The dress worn by Queen Victoria at a ball on the evening before her wedding. It was of white faille trimmed with frills of silver net and white satin bows. Drawing by P. Stevenson./***London Museum*

Below left: **A wedding dress of satin worn about 1830. The skirt is covered with embroidered net (run work) and a dress of moiré trimmed with fringing./***Victoria and Albert Museum*

A French marriage at St Roch, Paris. /*Mary Evans Picture Library*

Above: **Preparing for the ceremony, circa 1865. The bride wears a white cotton chemise and drawers, a corset and hinged wire crinoline frame, and white satin wedding boots. Drawing by Philippa Archer.**

Right: **A fashionable golden-buff wedding dress, 1838. Drawing by P. Stevenson from a dress in the London Museum.**

Left: **A bride dressed for the ceremony, circa 1850. Note the small oranges in her wreath and the bouquet-holder. Drawing by Philippa Archer.**

Below: **A white satin crinoline dress, trimmed with pleated ribbon and white roses. Drawing by P. Stevenson./***The Englishwoman's Domestic Magazine*

Right: **The wedding party at Mrs Byers, 1851. Drawn by John Leech for** *Illustrated London News.*/*Mary Evans Picture Library*

Below: **A factory owner presents a clock to the newlyweds. Taken from** *The British Workman*, **1856.**/*Mary Evans Picture Library*

Left: **A High Society Marriage. The Marquis of Westminster's daughter married at Motcomb in 1877. An ox was roasted whole and the village festivities lasted for days.**

Below: **The bridegroom jibbing at the post, 1858.**/*Mary Evans Picture Library*

The Matrimonial Hurlingham!

Far left, above: **The shooting party, circa 1870.**/*Punch's Pocket Book*

Far left, below: **The Honeymoon: Augustus makes the tea for the first month of his marriage, 1850. Drawing by John Leech.**/*Mary Evans Picture Library*

Left: **A white wedding dress of corded silk, with satin bows, lace, and trimmings, worn with a wreath of orange blossom, 1870. Drawing by P. Stevenson.**

Above: **Gallant rescue off the Bachelor Rocks, circa 1870.**/*Punch's Pocket Book*

Below: **A Quaker wedding, 1881. Margaret, daughter of Rt Hon John Bright MP marries Dr John Cash. A poem written especially for the occasion was read after the ceremony: "I, John, take friend Margaret for my wife, To be loving and faithful, while God gives us life . . ./No vows to the simple sweet promise lend force,/Yet who ever heard of a Quaker divorce?"**

Far left: **A wedding dress of about 1885 with an interesting veil arrangement.**

Above left: **A French bisque doll dressed as a bride, circa 1874.**/*Victoria and Albert Museum*

Above: **An English wax doll dressed as a bride, circa 1880.**/*Victoria and Albert Museum*

Left: **Signing the register, 1891. A drawing by Percy Tarant from** *Cassells Family Magazine.*/*Mary Evans Picture Library*

Below: **The supreme moment, circa 1890. The bride is ready for church.**

Right: **The front view of a wedding outfit showing an interesting veil and bodice arrangement, 1894. Drawing by P. Stevenson./***London Museum*

Far right: **The rear view of the same wedding outfit. Drawing by P. Stevenson./***London Museum*

Below: **The waning honeymoon, 1883.**

Left: **The bridesmaids from** *Cassells Family Magazine./Mary Evans Picture Library*

Below: **A dress in heavy satin with a huge bustle, 1884. Drawing by P. Stevenson.**

Bottom: **Princess May of Teck, later Queen Mary, choosing her trousseau, 1893.**

Right: **A wedding procession showing the bride in a dress of ivory satin with sleeves and yoke of lace worked in pearls. Her bouquet was of white lilacs tied with white velvet ribbon. Her train was held by the pages dressed in dark blue plush suits lined with gold satin. The bridesmaids wore white veiling with blue moire sashes, lace collars, and blue silk stockings and held gilt flower baskets from which they cast roses in the path of the bride.**

Below: **A marriage ceremony outside the bride's house in the Scottish Highlands, 1899. The simple wedding was followed by the couple and the guests marching off to the bridegroom's house, to the sound of the pipes.**/*Mary Evans Picture Library*

Far right: **The wedding morning. An advertisement for Sunlight Soap from** ***Myra's Journal*****, 1892.**

Appointed by
Special
Royal Warrant

Soap Makers
to Her Majesty
the Queen.

From the Painting by J. H. F. Bacon. *Exhibited at the Royal Academy, 1892.*

THE WEDDING MORNING.

What happy recollections the above Picture recalls to those who have helped a Bride with her toilet! Friends ask themselves, has the Bride a thorough knowledge of all the duties of a household, especially of that ever-recurring worry, Washing Day and Spring Cleaning? Does she know what

SUNLIGHT SOAP

can do? Does she know that for a few pence, without boiling or bleaching, she can, by using **SUNLIGHT SOAP**, have all the household linen washed at home and made to look white as snow and fresh as roses?

Happy is the bride who has been instructed in these matters, because it is on such simple household details as these that the future happiness and comfort of herself and husband must depend!

Right: **'Throwing the slipper' at the wedding of Princess Louise, a daughter of Queen Victoria, to the Marquess of Lorne in 1871.**/*Mary Evans Picture Library*

Below: **A smart wedding in Sierra Leone in the 1890s. The bride headed the procession in a bath chair followed by the bridesmaids carried in litters, while the men walked.**

Far right: **The marriage of Napoleon III of France to Eugenie. Her dress was described as being of spangled velvet, the high jacket bodice was decorated with diamonds and sapphires mixed with orange blossoms. The skirt was covered with English point lace and the veil was of Point d'Alençon.**/*Mary Evans Picture Library*

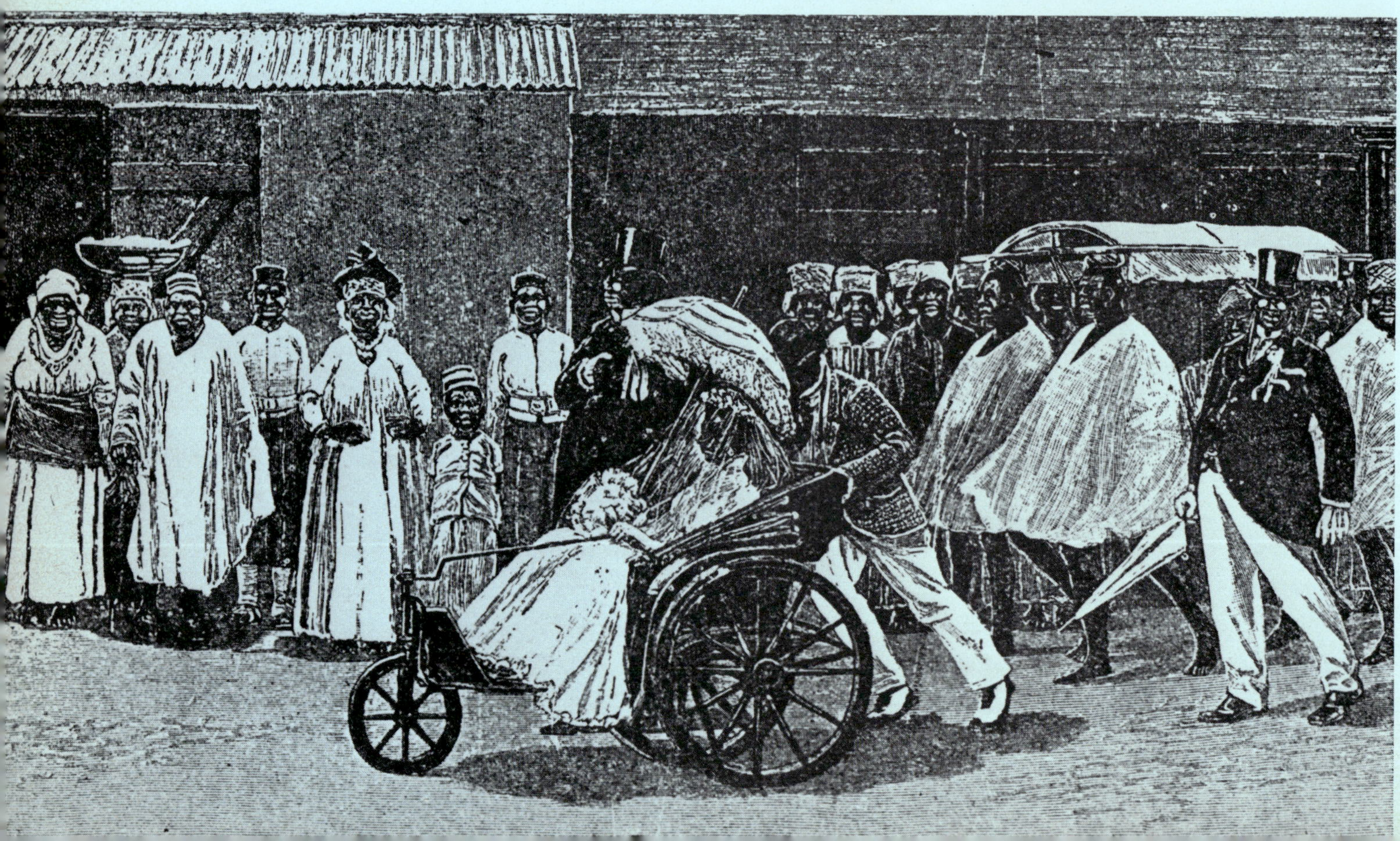

The wedding party at the photographers, 1870./*Mary Evans Picture Library*

A COMPTE
EN PUSANT.

1900~1910

Right: **The Archer-Eighteen wedding at Reading, circa 1909. The bride's maiden name was Eighteen and her family owned a number of fish shops, while the bridegroom's family, the Archers, were herring merchants. The fishing industry was then at its height.**

Top, centre right: **The bridesmaids of the Archer-Eighteen wedding wore deep red velvet frocks.**

Top, far right: **The bride's and groom's parents at the Archer-Eighteen wedding, circa 1909.**

Bottom, far right: **A country wedding in Devon in 1905. The girl clad in white and holding a bouquet was a bridesmaid. The bride wore a charming dress of nut brown, and a hat decorated with real ostrich feathers set off her auburn hair. An elegant parasol completed the outfit.**

RK VIEW

the Bride
William
Mother Father

Right: **A wedding in Exeter in 1909. The bridegroom, Mr F. R. Rowley, a former curator of the Royal Albert Memorial Museum, Exeter, and his bride. The bride's dress, of very soft white satin, was decorated with true lover's knots.**

Below: **Mr F. R. Rowley and his bride, Miss Jerman, with the family group in the garden. The younger women wore the then fashionable wide-brimmed hats while their seniors still wore the bonnets of a decade before.**

Left: **A fashionable London bride wearing the new high-waisted Regency-style dress of 1905./***The Queen*

Below left, below and next page: **Various Edwardian brides and their bridesmaids, whose weddings were described in great detail in** *The Queen* **and other fashion magazines; the articles were copiously illustrated by drawings and photographs.**

MISS WHITTING'S WEDDING GOWN AND BRIDESMAIDS' DRESS.
Made by Mmes. Mannering and Hinchliffe, 11A, Welbeck-street, Cavendish-square, W.)

MISS DYER-EDWARDES' WEDDING AND BRIDESMAIDS' GOWNS.
(Wedding Gown made by Russell and Allen. Bridesmaids' Gowns made by Mme, Kate Ker-Lane, 1, High-street, Kensington,)

MISS HOBHOUSE'S WEDDING AND TRAVELLING GOWNS.

MISS D'ARCY CLARK'S WEDDING GOWN AND BRIDESMAIDS' DRESS.
(Made by Caroline Sear, 25, Alfred-place West, South Kensington, S.W.)

MISS NAYLOR'S WEDDING AND BRIDESMAIDS' GOWNS. (Made by Mme. Clapham, Kingston-square, Hull.)

MISS WHITTING'S TRAVELLING COSTUME.

LADY EVELYN WELLESLEY'S BRIDESMAIDS' DRESS.

Far left, above and below: **A typical Edwardian bridesmaid's dress and bride's travelling costume.**

Far left: **A Liberty's satin embroidered teagown. Drawing by P. Stevenson.**

Left: **The bride and bridegroom at an Edwardian wedding, circa 1906.**

Below: **The family group at the same wedding, circa 1906. The broad-brimmed bridesmaids' hats are particularly distinctive.**

Below: **Mr and Mrs Backhouse Archer, a Norfolk couple in 1914.**

1910~1930

Above right: **Mr and Mrs Backhouse Archer's wedding group in 1914.**

Below right: **An elegant family group in 1913.**

Right: **A bridesmaid's dress in pink and white striped linon and white organdie by Renée.**/*Vogue*

Far right: **A bridesmaid's dress in pink muslin trimmed with beads and ostrich feathers with a pink and silver striped sash, by Beer, 1919.**/*Vogue*

Bottom centre: **A little bridesmaid in a light beige dress with pink silk roses, 1919.**/*Vogue*

Bottom right: **A white tulle bridesmaid's dress over a charmeuse foundation trimmed with embroidery of encrusted roses and black velvet ribbon, by Lanvin, 1919./ Drawings by P. Stevenson.**/*Vogue*

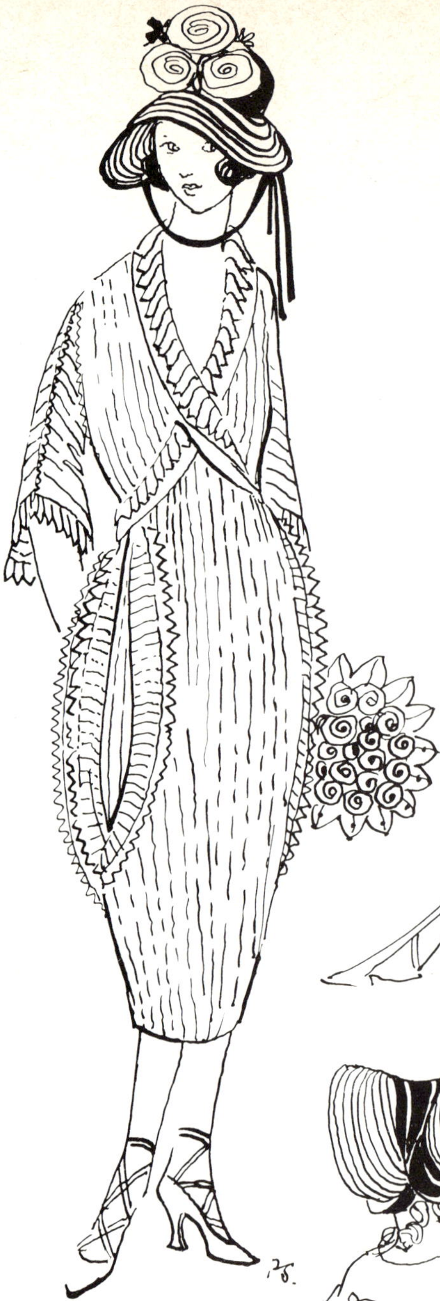

Above: **The bride was given away by her father.**/*Gazette du Bon Ton*

Below: **Dressing the bride 1913.**/*Gazette du Bon Ton*

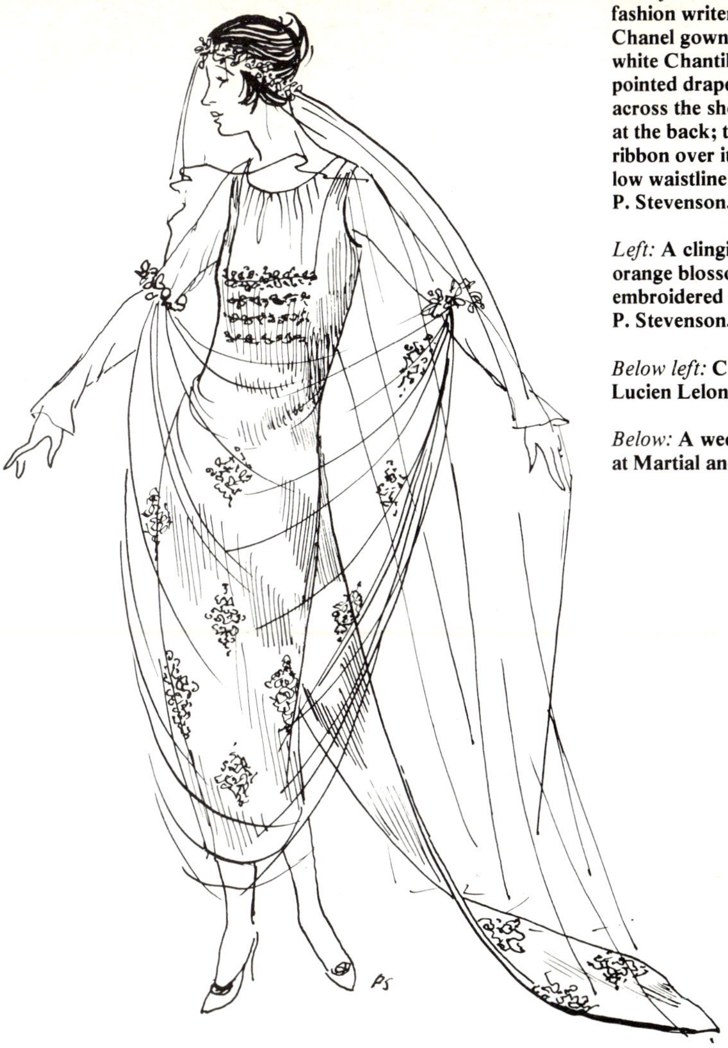

Far left: **In the words of a contemporary fashion writer "When one marries in a Chanel gown, one swathes white satin with white Chantilly lace which falls into pointed drapery at the sides and floats across the shoulders into an airy manteau at the back; then one ties white satin ribbon over it all to make the inevitable low waistline!" 1919. Drawing by P. Stevenson./***Vogue*

Left: **A clinging gown of white satin, orange blossom and white silver-embroidered tulle, 1919. Drawing by P. Stevenson./***Vogue*

Below left: **Choosing the wedding dress at Lucien Lelong./***Femina*

Below: **A wedding dress on a mannequin at Martial and Armand./***Femina*

Above: **A Renaissance-style wedding dress by Poiret.**/*Femina*

Right: **A bride and her small bridesmaid by Molyneux, circa 1921.**/*Femina*

Below: **Waiting to congratulate the happy pair. Drawing by D. A. Marty, circa 1920**

Far right: **Brides and bridesmaids, circa 1920.**

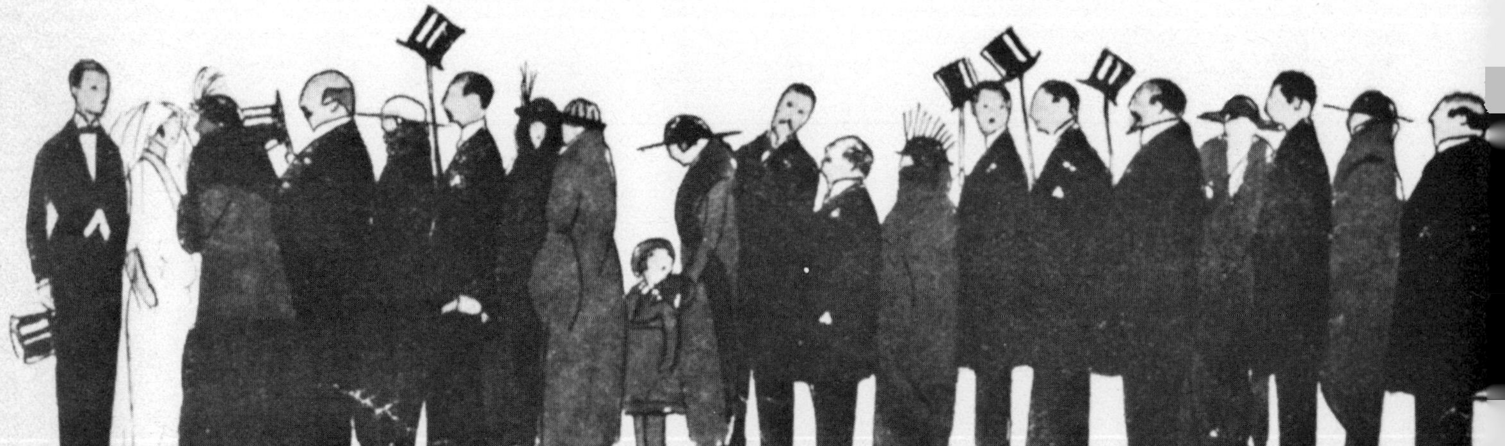

A group of two frocks that would be pretty for child bridesmaids. That on the left is of "fleur de France" simply trimmed with ruches of ribbon, while that on the right is of cachemirette embroidered with dots, the old-fashioned ruches being also of ribbon

ORANGE

NICOLE GROULT

DŒUILLET

The above wedding-dress is of panécla, crossed on one side and worn over a lace foundation. It is completed by a Court train in panécla, over which falls the long lace veil. On the right is a bridesmaid's toilette of Circé velvet, the corsage embroidered with a large motif of roses in different shades, a band of the same embroidery encircling the skirt. The hat is a simple capeline with a chain of cabochons surrounding the crown

NICOLE GROULT

In the group at the bottom of the page are two bridesmaids, the one on the left wearing French blue opéra satin, the skirt and Breton sleeves being outlined with black velvet, while the one on the right is in Nattier-blue panécla, the corsage being slightly draped and the skirt embroidered with large rose and black motifs. The bride wears a gown of silver lamé brocade, the top of the corsage being entirely of silver lace. The long tulle veil is held in place by a wreath of orange-blossom

A French-American wedding at Uzès, Gard, France./*Femina*

Right: **After the ceremony, a meal served in the courtyard of the chateau to friends and tenants.**/*Femina*

Below: **A drawing by P. Stevenson of the Duchesse showing her train edged with sable.**

Below right: **Photographed is the bride's mother-in-law, the Duchess de Uzès in embroidered velvet and sable.**

Below far right: **On the eve of the wedding, the American bride-to-be is presented by her fiance, the Duc de Crussol, to the inhabitants of Uzès from the balcony.**/*Femina*

A photograph of Queen Victoria's wedding dress from the London Museum.

Right: **A coloured engraving of a French bride and bridesmaid, circa 1885, from *Journal des Dames et des Demoiselles*. The bride carries a prayer book in preference to the traditional bouquet.**

Below: **A coloured engraving of a French wedding dress, in tarletan (a stiff gauze muslin), and English point lace, circa 1843.**

Carwiere imp Paris Bd. S. D. S. Reproduction interdite Abel Goubaud Edr Paris.

JOURNAL DES DAMES ET DES DEMOISELLES

ET BRODEUSE ILLUSTRÉE RÉUNIS

Bureaux de l'Administration, 33, Rue Blaes Bruxelles

Toilettes de Mad.lle Adelphine KŒNIG 31 r. St Augustin. Tissus et Foulards de la Mon LEHOUSSEL 1 rue Auber.

Parfums Cosmétiques et Savons de GUERLAIN parfumeur 15 r. de la Paix Paris.

Above: **The blacksmith officiates at a wedding over the anvil at Gretna Green.**/*Barnaby's Picture Library*

Below: **Le mariage au château, circa 1913.**/*Gazette du Bon Ton.*

Matching wedding and engagement rings designed by Jocelyn Burton./*De Beers Diamond Mines Ltd*

A matching wedding and engagement ring and others designed by Jocelyn Burton./*De Beers Diamond Mines Ltd*

A wedding dress in Edwardian style, using three tones of oyster, peach, and coffee silk satin, and chiffon with hand-dyed lace. Designed by Trisha Kerr-Cross and worn at her own wedding in 1972 to Roy Burge.

Right: A wedding group in which the page is obviously enjoying being a Scotsman for the day. The bride's dress is in georgette and guipure lace, and the bridesmaid is wearing fine polyester cotton printed with rosebuds./*Moss Bros*

Wedding dress of ivory satin-backed crepe and ivory chiffon, worn by Margaret, daughter of Sir Arthur and Lady Eliot of Stobs. The veil was once the property of the Queen of Rumania and is over 100 years old. Dress by Peter Lewis Crown of Lachasse./*Tomas Jaski Ltd*

Left: **The amateur wedding photographer, circa 1921.**

Below: **The wedding guests choosing velvet dresses, 1920;** ***(left to right)*** **a dress in red velvet, another of embroidered velvet, and a third in black satin and velvet.** */Femina*

Bottom: **In French churches the beadle led the wedding procession;** ***(right to left)*** **the bride's mother in tears and silver-grey crêpe satin, two guests in velvet with jet embroidery, and the beadle. Drawings by Erickson.***/Femina*

"May I present my Fiancé ?", 1920./*Femina*

"May you be very happy!", circa 1921./*Femina*

The honeymooners steal quietly away./*Femina*

Left: **A country wedding procession in Brittany. Drawing by D. A. Marty, 1921.** */Femina*

Below: **Lord Louis Mountbatten's wedding in 1922 to the Hon Edwina Ashley, later Viceroy and Vicereine of India, and friends of Mahatma Gandhi.** */Femina*

Some items from the trousseau of Lady Elizabeth Bowes-Lyon by Mme Handley Seymour, 1923. Drawings by P. Stevenson./*Courtesy of Vogue*

Left: **A pale yellow crêpe-de-chine blouse with a hat trimmed with grey and green ribbon.**

Below: **A green flannel coat** *(left)* **decorated with Egyptian motifs in black and silver;** *(right)* **a coat in white kid.**

Below left: **A grey wool jacket worn with a yellow straw hat and black velvet ribbon. Hats by Zyrot et Cie.**

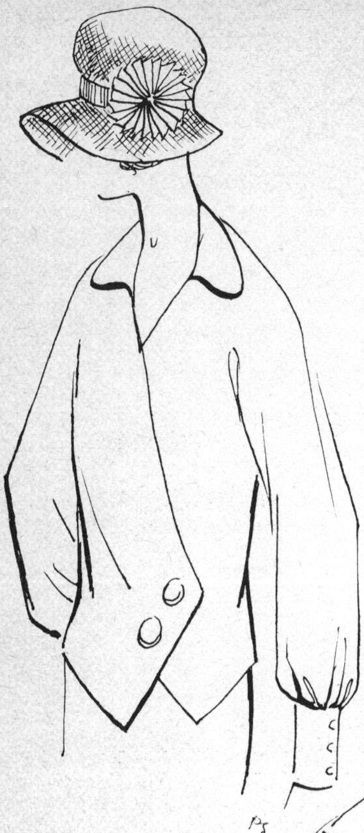

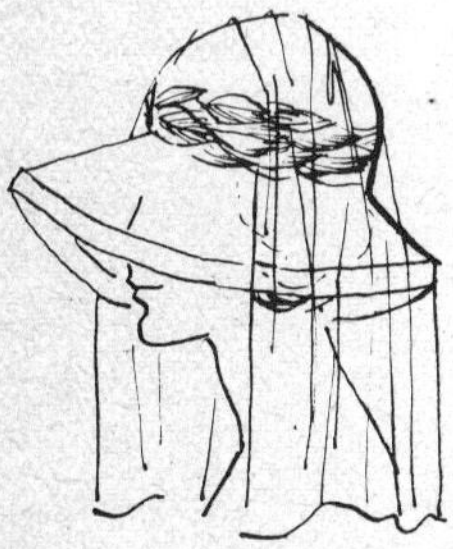

Above right: **Queen Elizabeth, the Queen Mother's wedding dress by Mme Handley Seymour in ivory chiffon moiré with a train from the waist. It was decorated with bands of silver lace, embroidered with silver thread, pearls and irridescent white beads. The fine old lace veil, lent by Queen Mary, was kept in place by a coronet of leaves with white roses and orange flowers at each side. The Queen Mother, then Lady Elizabeth Bowes-Lyon, was married to the Duke of York, later George VI, in April 1923.**

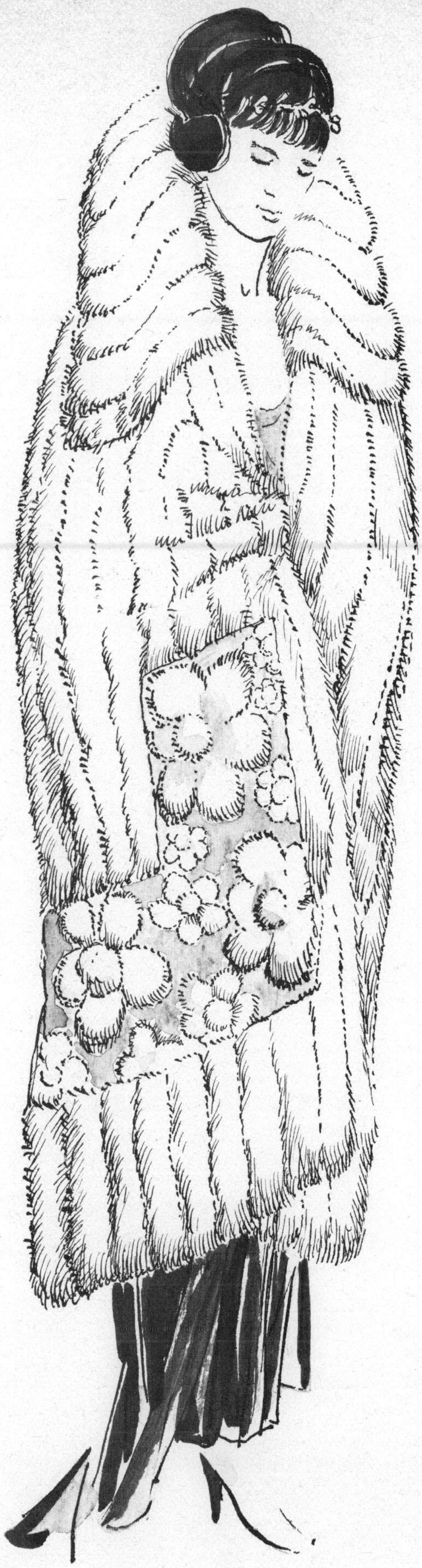

Far left: **An evening wrap by Uphely, of tail-less ermine, decorated with ermine flowers on corner panels of white velvet broche. It has a pocket but no sleeves.**

Left: **An evening wrap of gold imperator silk trimmed with sable.**

1930~1960

Below: **An Exeter wedding group, June 1930. The bridesmaids' dresses were of cream lace worn with cream hats; the child's dress, in Kate Greenaway style , was of pale green muslin.**

Right: **The bride's dress was of ivory chiffon velvet worn with a tulle veil and a wreath of Victorian orange blossom and the bouquet was of Harrisii lilies. The wreath flowers were wax, and the jewellery 18th century paste.**

Items from Princess Marina's trousseau by Molyneux, 1934. Drawings by P. Stevenson./*by courtesy of Vogue*

Below: **A pale green dress, with a belt of dark green sequins and a white ermine cape.**

Right: **The wedding dress designed by Molyneux for Marina, Duchess of Kent, married in 1934. The dress was in lamé with a raised floral design in silver and a long court train of the same lamé. A long tulle veil was held in place by a pearl and diamond tiara belonging to Princess Marina's grandmother, the Grand Duchess Vladimir of Russia. Drawing by P. Stevenson.**/*Vogue*

Far right: **A dress of apricot lamé shot with silver threads worn with a short cape jacket.**

Above: (Top left) **a black satin dress, with a sash of red crepe lined with silver;** *(top centre)* **an almond green coat and dress. The coat is trimmed with nutria;** *(centre right)* **a Scottish plaid coat and skirt in shades of beige, yellow, blue, green and red;** *(bottom)* **a black woollen suit, high shirred and corded collar.**

Top right: **A black velvet dress.**

Centre right: **An informal indoor gown of gold and silver.**

Right: **A black woollen coat trimmed with astrakhan.**

Items from Princess Marina's trousseau by Molyneux, 1934. Drawings by P. Stevenson./*Vogue*

Right: **A golden velvet coat** *(left)* **and skirt, trimmed with blue fox worn with a silver lamé blouse;** *(centre)* **a pink dress and red jacket with pink sleeves trimmed with one pink and one red chrysanthemum;** *(right)* **a dress in two shades of blue. The dress is in dark blue, with a turned-back collar and a lower part of the sleeves in pale blue.**

Below: **A wedding dress of satin showing cutwork embroidery and net veil, circa 1937.**/*Barnaby's Picture Library*

Left: **A dress and beaded tiara-like headdress of the late thirties. Note the bride's make-up.**/*Barnaby's Picture Library*

Below: **A dress of brocade and net made in 1949 similar to Christian Dior's bridal dress named 'Fidelity'. The Dior dress was in plain white satin and tulle. Drawing by P. Stevenson.**

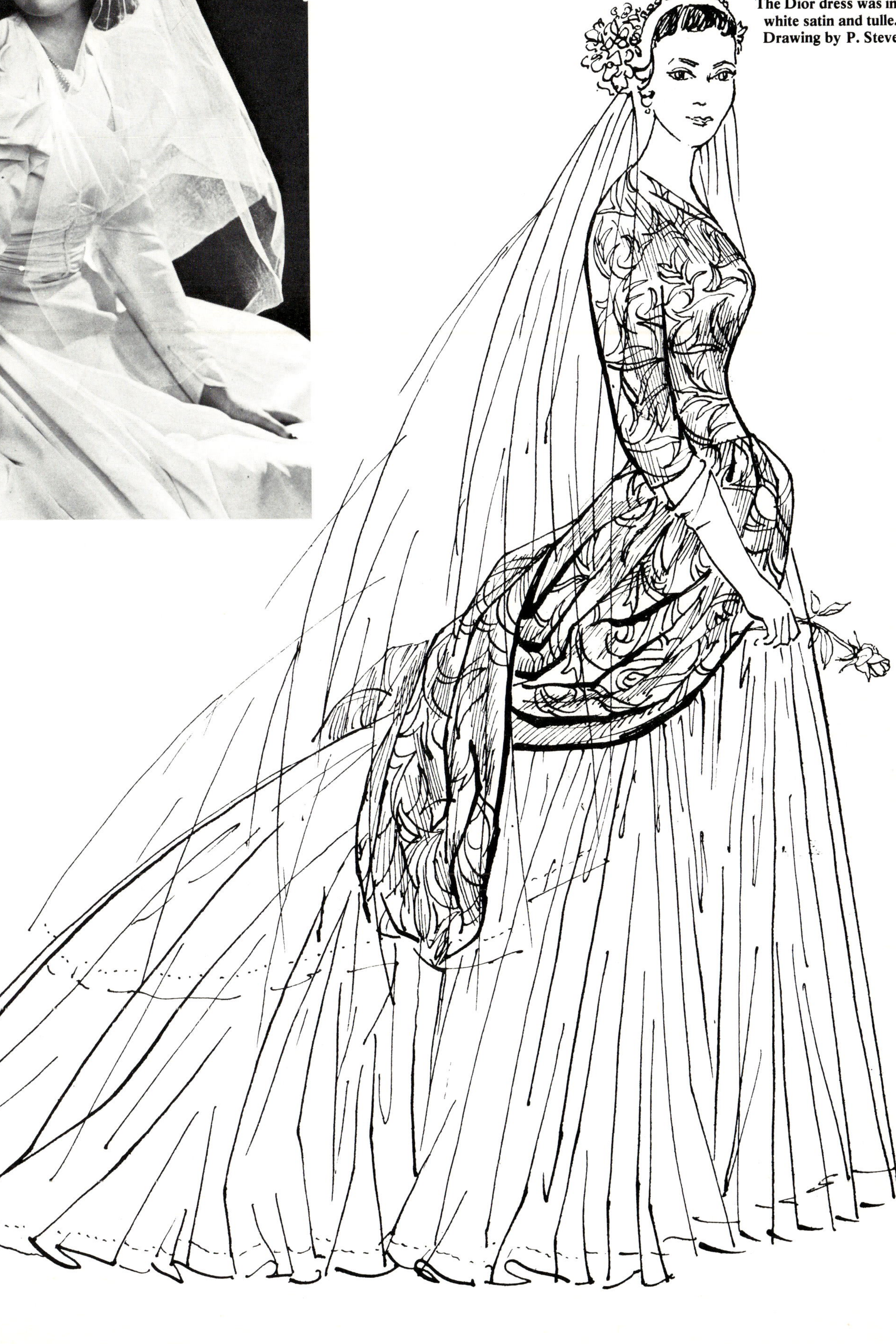

Right: **A model dress made to order in 1946 using material purchased before clothes rationing. Drawing by P. Stevenson.**

Far right: **A skimpy readymade dress of about the same date needing between 10-15 coupons. Drawing by P. Stevenson.**

R.B.1
15
MINISTRY OF FOOD
SERIAL NO.
BG 866065
1952-1953
RATION BOOK
(GENERAL)
Surname
Initials
Address
IF FOUND RETURN TO ANY FOOD OFFICE
FOOD OFFICE CODE No.
NM--D
1-11

Above left: **Cover of a Ration Book.**

Above: **Make-do and Mend, 1942. An attractive going-away hat and fur tie made from a black cap, the peak having been dispensed with, and trimmed with parts of a fur coat which was being remodelled of seal dyed leopard. The tie was made from parts surrounding the arm. Designed and made by Joseph Wright.**

Left: **Two dresses needing about 7 coupons each, which could be used for brides or bridesmaids, and be worn after the wedding. One girl wears a crownless, homemade hat. Drawing by P. Stevenson.**

Wedding dress worn by Miss Thomasson in 1959 in pure silk satin, created by Peter Lewis Crown at Lachasse, London.

Above: **A wedding group at Ealing, 1947. Note the square shoulders and hats.**

Left: **Dress made in Liberty's own workroom for the finale of 1949-50 fashion show, with an original pearl Juliet cap and silk net veil. Kindly loaned by Mrs Garnons-Williams.**/*Peter Johansen*

1960~1970

Right: **A design and drawing by Bill Gibb for his Autumn 1973 collection. The dress and coat were in silk taffeta, the coat sleeveless and the dress embroidered with flowing sleeves and embroidered cuffs. The veil, which had a guipure edging, was attached to the jewelled headdress. Designed and drawn by Bill Gibb**

Far right: **Firefly — Faith Sole — the 18-year old girl who was named as the superstar model of the seventies, married fashion photographer Mike Taylor at Caxton Hall in April 1970. The ceremony was a colourful affair — the bride wore a £300 outfit with a pair of handmade pink and silver shoes, while the groom wore a green and wine-coloured satin suit with flame-throwing dragons on each lapel./***Keystone Press*

Below right: **The ten Japanese couples who flew from Tokyo to Vaud in Switzerland pictured after their collective marriage ceremony at the Church of Lutry./***Keystone Press*

Below: **A wedding dress, designed by Bill Gibb for his Spring 1973 collection, was augmented by a waistcoat and streamers of flowers in soft pastel shades which complement the print. The veil was replaced by small bunches of flowers over each ear. Designed and drawn by Bill Gibb**

Left: Actress Jenny Kerna after her marriage to Brian Lidstone at Caxton Hall Registry Office in March 1973./*Keystone Press*

Below: A wedding dress commissioned by Liberty's in white Italian crepe with large leg o'mutton sleeves and flowing inset gores forming a train. All the seams were inset with white guipure lace. The long wispy veil worn with it was attached to a jewelled cap. Spring 1974. Designed and drawn by Bill Gibb.

Far left: **A wedding procession to the accompaniment of a wind-up gramophone after the service at the Pentecostal Church in Western Province, Kenya.** */Barnaby's Picture Library*

Above left: **Clouds of rose petals, instead of rice as in the old days.***/Barnaby's Picture Library*

Above: **A charming oriental bride in a western style bouffant veil.***/Barnaby's Picture Library*

Left: **Of course the sun shone all day when these couples from all over France were married on St Médard's day — St Médard is the patron saint of umbrellas! Here they are in Paris after a reception given in their honour by the press.** */Keystone Press*

Far left: **Little bridal attendants at a Southgate wedding.**/*Barnaby's Picture Library*

Centre left: **Kissing is the fashion at an American wedding and a bride may collect more than 200. Here, a bridesmaid is busy collecting them.**/*Barnaby's Picture Library*

Left: **Signing the register after the ceremony.**/*Barnaby's Picture Library*

Below: **The wedding Mass after the ceremony.**/*Barnaby's Picture Library*

Right: **Reading messages and telegrams at the wedding breakfast.**/*Barnaby's Picture Library*

Below: **A bride of 72 photographed at her wedding with her bridegroom of 30 in the church at Gravellona Toce, Italy in October 1972. She was a famous Italian actress and he was a poet and actor.** /*Keystone Press*

Left: **A modern Jewish wedding. Men sit on one side of the synagogue, women on the other. The bride wears white while the bridegroom wears a hat and a prayer shawl.**/*Barnaby's Picture Library*

Below: **Canon Collin's youngest son, Mark, was married at St Paul's Cathedral, by his father, to an American girl, Miss Anne Faulkner. He wore a black velvet suit and the bride was dressed in a high-waisted Empire style gown. The older bridesmaids wore dresses of Indian fabric.**/*Keystone Press*

A wedding dress designed in 1970 by Gina Fratini of pure silk organza over creamy-primrose soft taffeta lining, trimmed with old hand-made lace, and with slotted primrose satin ribbons and pin-tucking. Now part of the Cecil Beaton collection at the Victoria and Albert Museum. Drawing by P. Stevenson.

Left: **An ex-Royal Marine who lost both legs in a Belfast bomb explosion photographed after his marriage to his childhood sweetheart at St Mary's Church, Widford, Chelmsford, May 1974.** */Keystone Press*

Below: **A lovely hat worn by a pretty London alderman at her wedding in May 1974 at St Pancras Town Hall.** */Keystone Press*

Right: **A classical white satin dress by Peter Lewis Cown at Lachasse with a polo-neckline and circular train. The outfit which was embroidered on the high-waisted bodice, hemline and train was worn by Miss Virginia Cave.**
/Archie Parker

Small bridal attendants dresses designed by Julia Tse, 1974; *(far left)* white broderie anglaise dress with cape sleeves edged with lace, three pleats each side with pink, pale blue and green 'Maypole' ribbons laced through; *(centre left)* pleated white lawn dress with red and green embroidery and green 'Maypole' ribbons inset in each pleat. Flowers are attached to the ribbon ends; *(left)* knitted white mercerised cotton dress with round yoke. Pink, pale green and yellow ribbons lace through the holes to form pleats on the bodice.

Below left: A dress designed by Trisha Kerr-Cross and worn by her at her wedding in 1972.

Below: The medieval influence can be seen in this dress of dark green velvet, appliquéd with silk in three colours and a piping of yellow silk printed with green to match the green of the dress. The same silk covers the buttons. The Juliet cap is made up in sections of green velvet and yellow and green striped silk. Designed, printed and made by Sophie Keith-Roach and worn by her at her wedding in 1974.

Below: **A dress in re-embroidered lace and white silk faille with a train, worn at her wedding, by Mrs Fay Newberry, designed by Peter Lewis Crown. Drawing by P. Stevenson.**

Right: **A dress of white silk with slim fitting bodice and peg-top skirt, with a train and clouds of veiling, worn by Miss Caroline Grant. Designed by Peter Lewis Crown at Lachasse./***F. Ziranek*

Far right: **The dress of paper-white silk faille with a bouquet of lilies of the valley and a train shaped like an arum lily was worn by the Hon Jane Leverhulme when she married Mr Algernon Heber-Percy. She also wore the family diamonds. The dress was designed by Peter Lewis Crown at Lachasse./***Swaebe*

Right: **A wedding dress and textile design by Leonie Mae Tucker. The dress was in white silk organza over pale beige satin, the design becoming progressively darker towards the bottom. The transparent yoke was surrounded by three circular layers of silk organza, shading from white through beige to sepia. Pale beige ribbons gathered the sleeves at the wrists. The dress was worn with a bonnet of beige satin decorated by a tiny frill and eye veil. Drawing by Leonie Mae Tucker.**

Centre right: **A dress in Tudor style worn by Miss Rose Ellerton. The apron front was emphasised by a wide band of velvet, and the veil, embroidered with a trellis design in seed pearls, fell from a Tudor headdress. Design by Peter Lewis Crown of Lachasse.**/*Belgrave Press*

Far right: **Surgeon-Commander and Mrs McEwan leave the church with a naval guard of honour. The bride wore a shocking pink dress covered with eight layers of organza, the top being white, with a white raised rosebud motif. The nine layers of material gave the effect of pink mother-of-pearl. Designed by Peter Lewis Crown at Lachasse.**/*Belgrave Press*

Below: **A wedding dress of striped white Tootal cotton, opening in front to show ruffled trousers spangled with diamanté. The trousers were attached to the front panels of the skirt underneath. White cotton ruffs trimmed the neck and sleeves and the model carried a muff of the same cotton tied with diamante ribbon. This dress was shown at an exhibition of future trends in the design section of the Clothing Institute in the mid-sixties. Designed by Peter Lewis Crown. Drawing by P. Stevenson**

Right: **A brides dress in silk and silk organza with hand-made lace inserted into the yoke and trimming the sleeves and hemline. Note the slotted ribbon trimming and the hand-embroidered old lace veil. Made exclusively for Liberty's 1974 collection by Trisha Kerr-Cross.**
/Peter Johansen

Left: **A bridal dress made from an embroidered sari length of cotton showing Liberty's continued interest in oriental fabrics. Made exclusively for the 1974 collection by Raksha Tandon.**/*Peter Johansen*

Below: **A beautifully cut dress of heavy silk with a concealed box-pleated panel in front. It had a train, and a diamond tiara held the very long veil in place. The veiled bride was Miss Lullaway photographed entering the church. Designed by Peter Lewis Crown at Lachasse.**/*Belgrave Press*

A silk organza bridal gown with fine pin tucks and with ribbon streamers threaded through slotted lace. Flowers emphasised the collar, yolk and cuffs. An old lace veil was held in place by flowers. Made exclusively for Liberty's by Patricia Miller./*Peter Johansen*

"A Nice Idea"

Nice Idea. An attractive modern idea dealing with all aspects of wedding stationery in various colours./*Nice Idea*

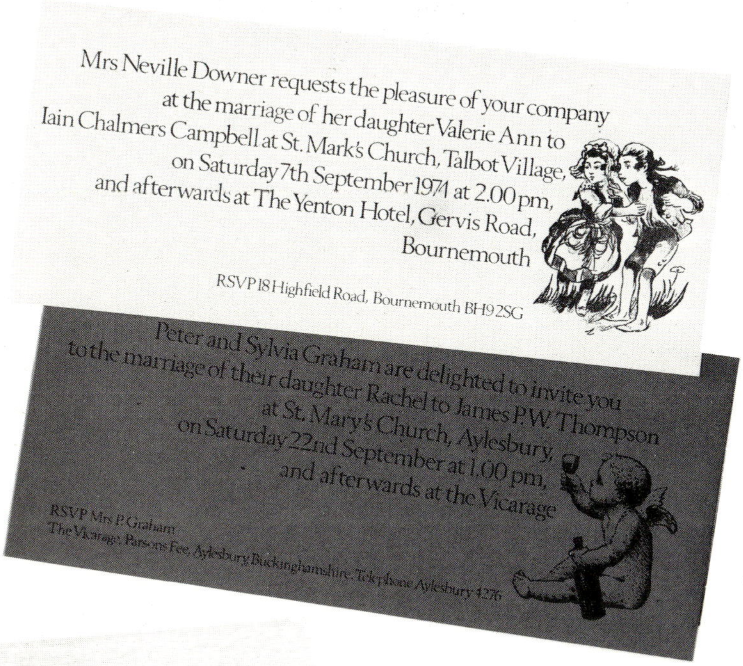

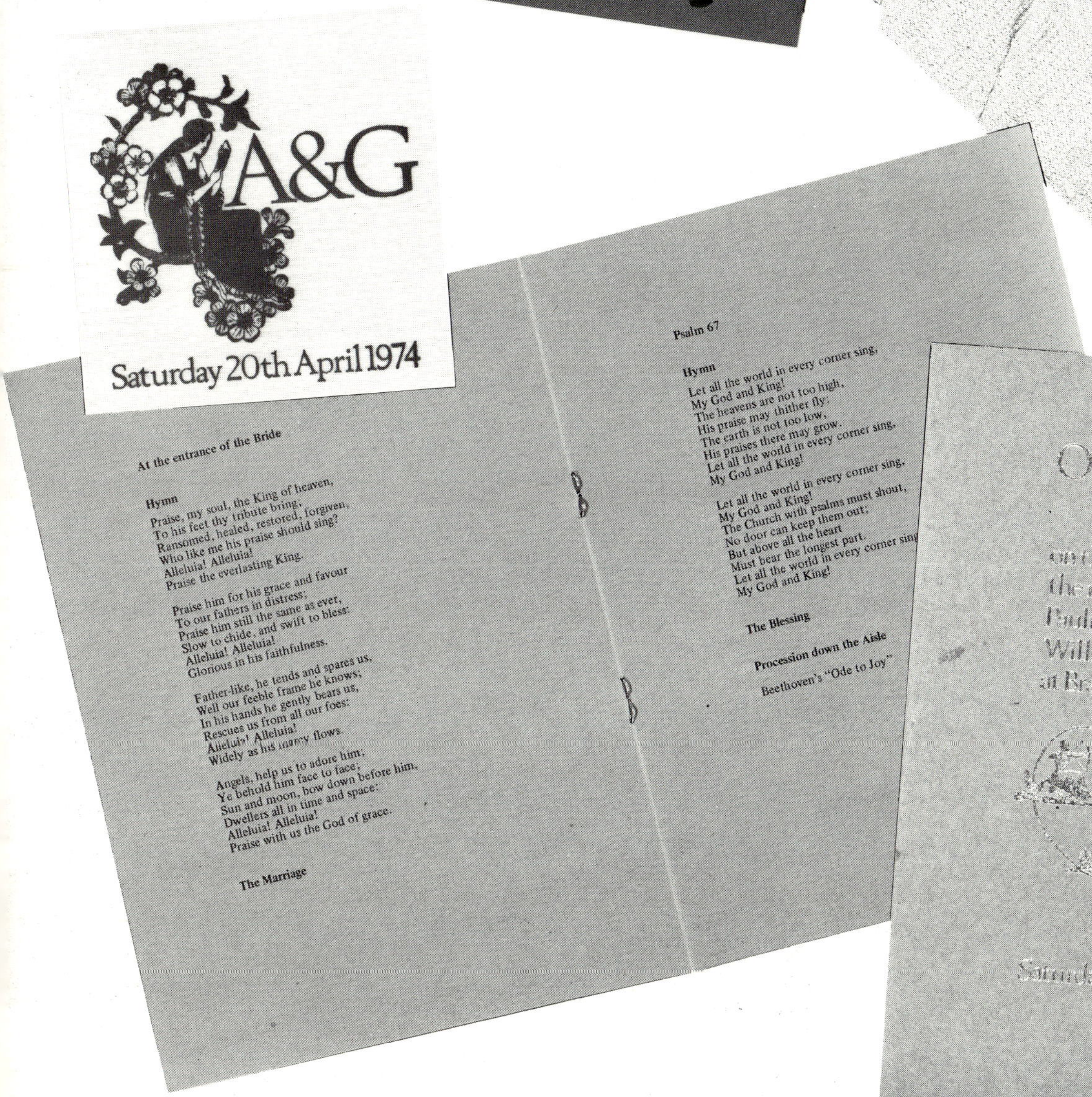

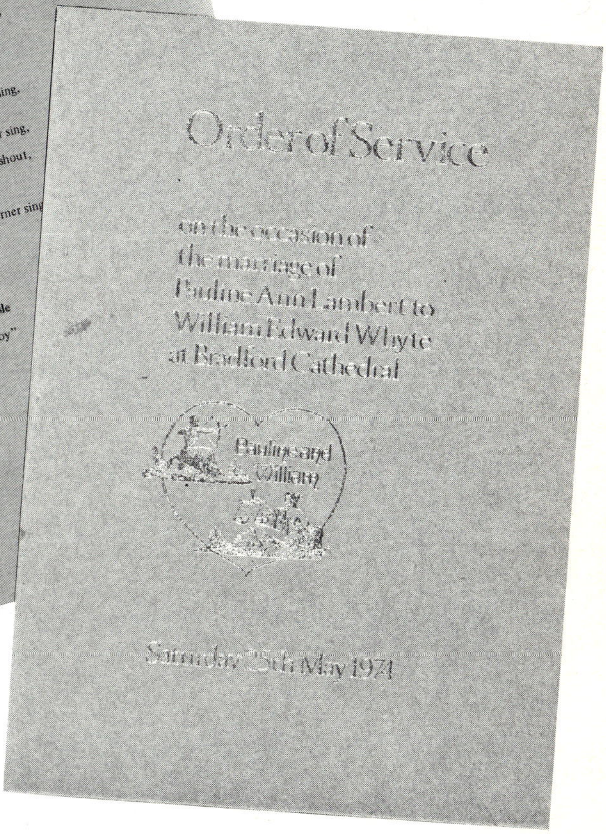

The Hiring

Marry in Haste? Don't worry, you can hire the lot!

Far left: **The perfect bride's dress for a real country-style wedding in vanilla Dacron and cotton. The full skirt has a pinafore overskirt, tied at the back with a party-dress bow. The bodice, cuffs and hem of the dress are edged in a generous band of white crochet lace. A little lace mob cap, ringed with flowers, completes the fresh country look. The bridesmaid's empire-line dress is in a crisp check gingham with spot organza full sleeves caught in a frilled cuff with a tiny gingham bow, and is worn with a charming white lace bonnet. Photograph March 1974./***Moss Bros*

Left: **A model dress in white organza and corded Chantilly lace and appliquéd flowers scattered over the full skirt and sleeves, and worn with a tiara. It shows the return to romantic Victorian styles. March 1973./***Moss Bros*

Above: **A white or cream georgette dress suitable for a church or registry office wedding, and worn with a cream hat with a frothy lace brim and trimmed with full blown roses and floating ribbon. March 1974./***Moss Bros*

The Trousseau

The Victorian Trousseau
(a) **Chemise usually worn under the corset.**
(b) **American wire bustle, circa 1887.**
(c) **Corset, circa 1880.**
(d) **Nightgown and** (e) **flannel knickers.**
(f) **Sanitary combinations.**
(g) **Knickers, circa 1880.**
(h) **Red flannel open drawers (2 legs on a band) from Massachusetts, circa 1880.**
(i) **Bustle, and petticoat of canvas stiffened with cane.**

The trousseau was probably an off-shoot of the dowry, which in earlier times was always provided by the bride's parents. When quite young a girl started to make and collect things for her 'bottom drawer', in which the necessities of future marriage were traditionally stored. A Victorian magazine records the following:

Preparation for Marriage
'An old maid recently died who left property to the value of nearly £8,000. She was all her lifetime getting ready to be married and had stored up 182 sheets, 63 coverlets, 50 blankets, 27 beds with 120lbs of feathers, 54 pillows, 52 handkerchiefs, and numerous other articles'.

In the Victorian age of prudery, however, the collection of underclothing was not always undertaken without a guilt feeling. In the fascinating *History of Underclothes* the authors C. Willett and Phillis Cunnington, tell of a young lady exclaiming at the prospect of marriage: 'How awful it must be to be seen by one's husband in one's petticoats!' And there was the bride who wrote to her Mama that she was so horrified by the sight of her husband's nightshirts that she was spending the honeymoon 'making him nice long nightgowns, so that I shan't be able to see any of him.'

Victorian underclothes were certainly daunting. Brides could not really enjoy their trousseaux until the 20th century changed attitudes, and frills, ribbons and laces and insertions appeared on every garment to which it was possible to attach them.

One Victorian women's journal advised its readers that a trousseau should be compiled like this:

'We have been repeatedly asked to describe, at one time, what house linen, at another, what underlinen, would be considered sufficient for the wedding trousseaux of brides in the middle-class society; that is to say, those who may soon have command of incomes ranging from £400 to £600 a year. For such ladies we now present, if we may use the term, a complete 'bridal outfit'.

a.

b.

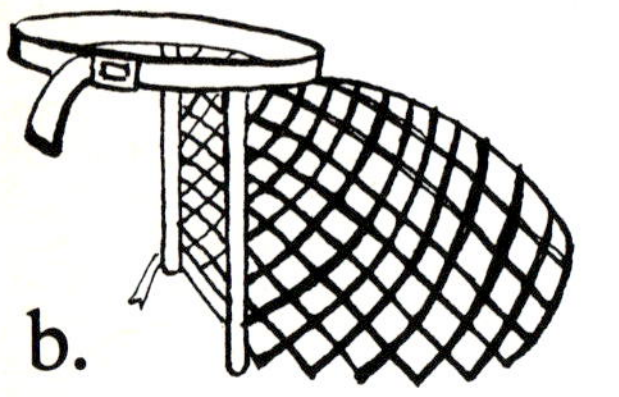

c.

d.

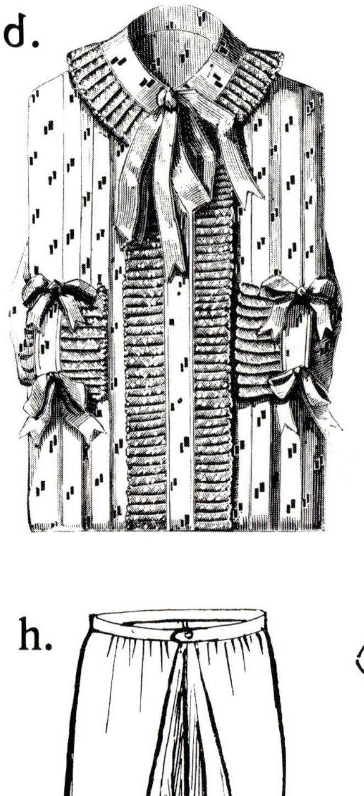

e.

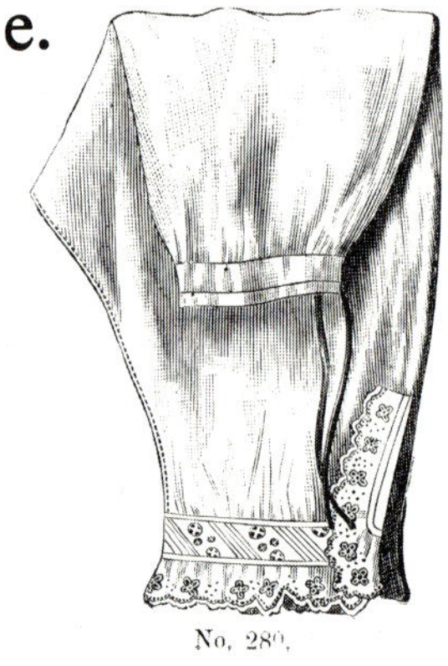

f.

g.

h.

i.

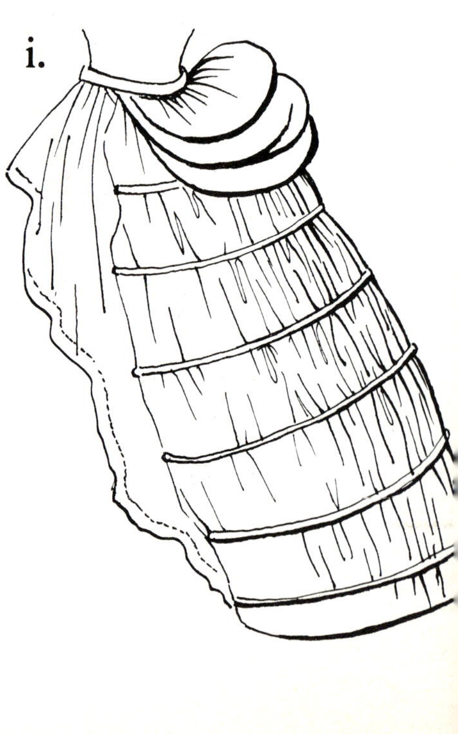

UNDER-LINEN.—Six flannel waistcoats (if these be worn) ; 6 pairs of flannel drawers (if these be worn) ; 12 chemises ; 12 pairs of drawers ; 12 pairs of cotton stockings ; 6 pairs of silk ditto; 6 pairs of winter ditto ; 4 pairs of stays ; 4 flannel petticoats for summer wear ; 4 ditto for winter wear ; 4 warm twill petticoats for wearing under crinolines ; 3 crinolines ; 3 simply tucked petticoats ; 3 with tucks and insertion ; 2 with frills one-eighth of a yard deep ; 2 handsome ditto with work and insertion ; 4 muslin petticoats for summer dresses ; 1 winter petticoat ; 1 under ditto ; 6 jacket bodices, trimmed with simple work ; 6 ditto, trimmed with insertion and work ; 12 nightdresses, variously trimmed ; 12 nightcaps, 6 simply trimmed and 6 richly trimmed.

ETCETERAS.—One dozen pocket handkerchiefs, plain ; 1 dozen ditto, hem-stitched ; 1 dozen ditto trimmed or embroidered ; 1 bridal ditto ; 12 plain linen sets of morning collars and cuffs ; 12 sets of fancy ditto, lace and muslin ; 1 black lace fichu or pelerine ; 1 white lace ditto, ditto ; 2 veils.

DRESSES, MANTELS, ETC.—Bridal dress ; 4 silk dresses, including a black one ; 1 moire antique ; 2 warm winter dresses ; 2 fancy material ditto ; 4 summer morning dresses ; 4 muslin ditto ; evening dresses according to requirement ; 1 flannel dressing-gown ; 1 breakfast dress ; 2 combing jackets ; Zouave jackets and vests, or chemisettes ; head-dresses, if required ; 1 Paisley shawl ; 1 black lace ditto ; 1 thick travelling shawl ; 1 ditto, ditto, rug ; silk mantles, cloth ditto, shawls, etc., for outdoor wear ; 2 sets of fur ; 1 umbrella ; 2 parasols ; 1 pair of goloshes ; boots, various ; shoes, ditto ; slippers, 2 pairs ; evening boots and shoes, if required ; 12 pair of gloves.

HOUSE-LINEN.—Six pairs of best sheets ; 6 pairs of medium ditto ; 2 pairs of fine ditto, with pin-stitched tops ; 4 pairs of servants' sheets ; 12 bolster-cases ; 6 pairs of trimmed pillow-cases ; 12 pairs of good linen ditto ; 6 pairs of servants' pillow-cases ; 6 dozen chamber towels ; 1 dozen Turkish ditto ; 2 dozen servants' ditto ; 18 toilet covers ; 8 full-sized dinner table-cloths ; 8 smaller, ditto, for breakfast ; 6 ditto, for kitchen use ; 4 sideboard-cloths ; 6 tray-cloths ; 24 full-sized table napkins ; 12 breakfast ditto ; 12 fringed d'oyleys ; 6 fish napkins ; 12 glass-cloths ; 12 tea-cloths ; 24 dusters—6 for drawing-room use ; 1 dozen rough brown kitchen cloths ; 8 round towels ; 12 knife-cloths.

By the end of the 19th century we read of coloured nightgowns with frills and ribbons and even of pyjamas; by then attractive underwear was no longer considered a sign of depravity. 'Americans and other ultra-smart folk', we are told 'are very fond of black silk or gauze nightgowns! But the true blue English fashion writer did not really recommend these for the trousseau, though she did concede that an underlying spirit of coquetry was permissible in a young and charming bride.'

In the 1920s a fascinating booklet produced by Maison L. Giraud (The White House) listed a series of seven trousseaux, ranging from 'Love in a cottage' to the 'Trousseau de luxe' and including 'Trousseau Fantasie', aimed at the artistic or Bohemian type of bride. Trousseaux remained fairly extensive until World War II and rationing. In the 1950s and with the invention of man-made fibres of all types it was once again possible to achieve the allure and seduction of Edwardian days, although, of course, the massive quantities of garments and articles of that period were never repeated.

Nowadays, the bride is often earning as much money as the bridegroom. Generally they choose together the things they want for their home, and the bride will buy her own lingerie.

The Edwardian Trousseau
(a) **Nightdress.**
(b) **Bust improvers.**
(c) **Corset cover and petticoat.**
(d) **Draws.**
(e) **Corset.**
(f) **Skirt knickers.**

a.

b.

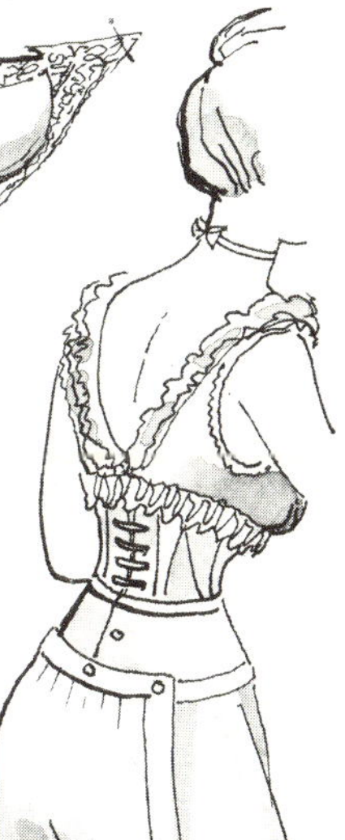
d.

e.

c.

f.

In the WARDROBE

NIGHTDRESSES ARE OF VARIOUS FORMS, MOST OF THEM HAVING NO SLEEVES. THE PETTICOAT HAS REAPPEARED

Combinations of rose voile, incrusted with Milanese lace and trimmed with ribbons and tiny roses cover a corset-belt of silk batiste

SEURRE

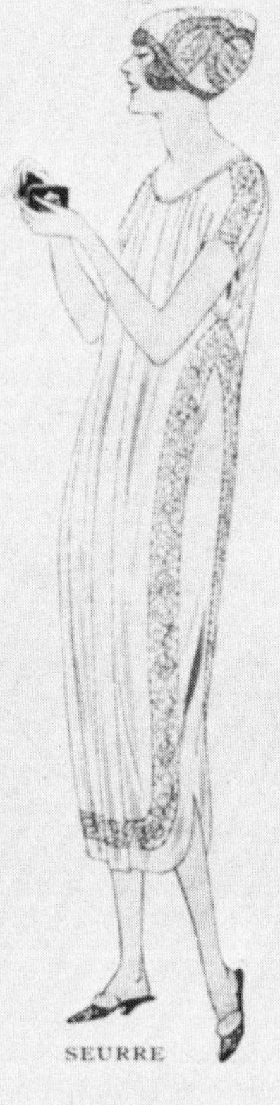

A pretty nightdress, gathered at the neck into a bias of the same material and trimmed with an insertion of Valenciennes

SEURRE

LANVIN

Above is a delightful négligé from Lanvin in flesh coloured voile cachemirette, the skirt striped with silver ribbon. The pretty casaquin, inspired by the peasant blouse, is soutached with silver and bordered with silver ribbon. Openwork decorates the top of the blouse

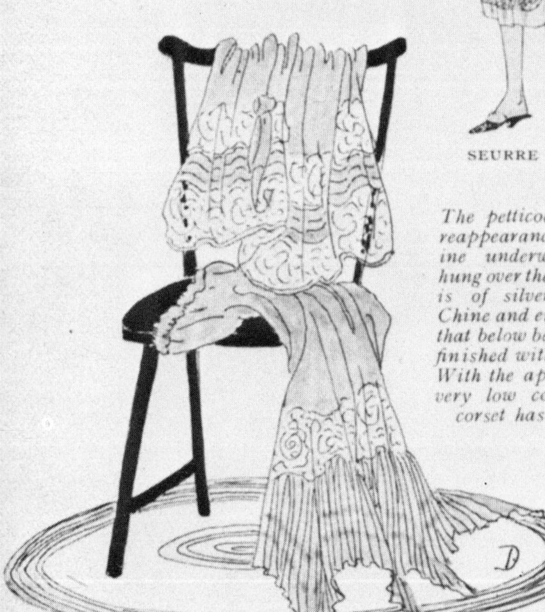

The petticoat has made its reappearance among feminine underwear. The one hung over the back of the chair is of silver grey crêpe de Chine and embroidered tulle, that below being of rose satin finished with a pleated frill. With the appearance of the very low corset the cache-corset has disappeared.

MARTIAL AND ARMAND

These two nighties are quite new in form, one having a corselet made with a yoke covering the top of the arms, the other being slit on the shoulders. That on the left is trimmed with gathered tulle, the other with hem-stitching

Far left: **Page from *Femina* showing a twenties trousseau.**

Left: **Elaborate silk pyjamas showing the twenties craze for things Oriental.** */Barnaby's Picture Library*

Below: **Peach crêpe-de-chine cami-knickers decorated with pale coffee lace, circa 1920.***/Barnaby's Picture Library*

Right and far right: **Negligé and petticoat in heavy satin and real lace from The White House.**

Below and bottom right: **The trousseau of the 1950s.**

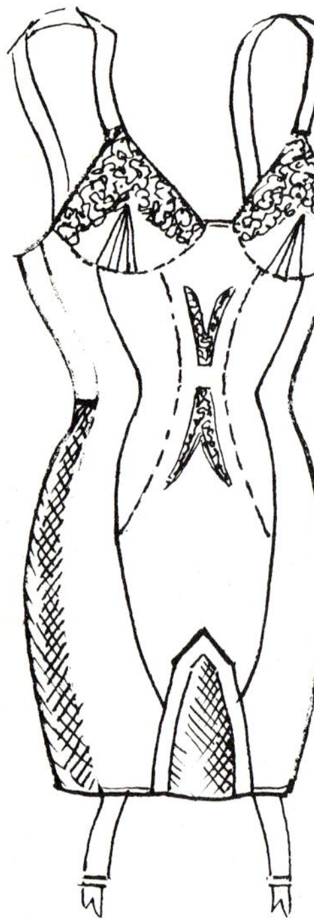

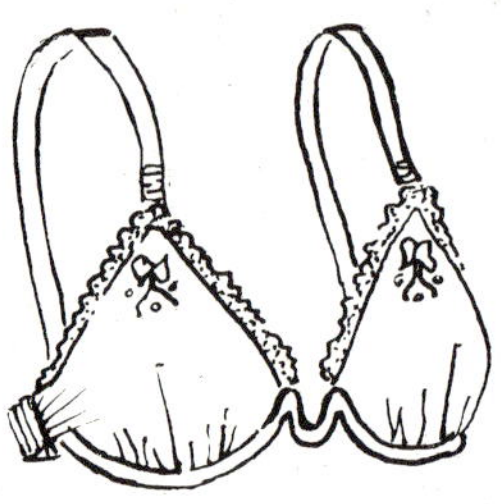

Below and bottom left: **Everything in nylon from The White House. Drawings by P. Stevenson**

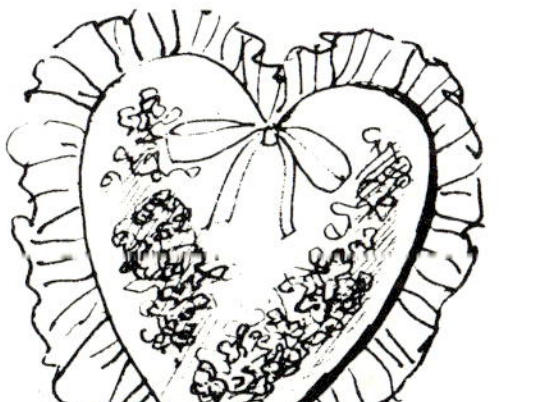

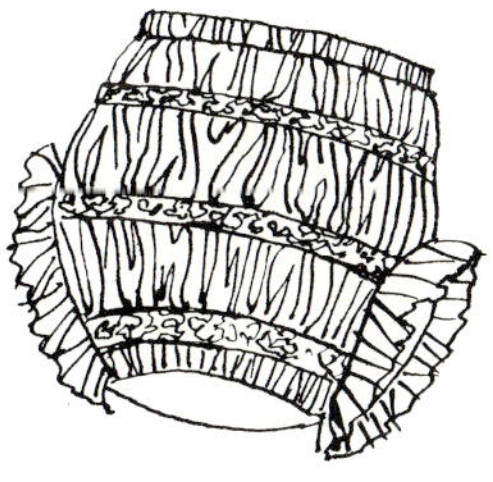

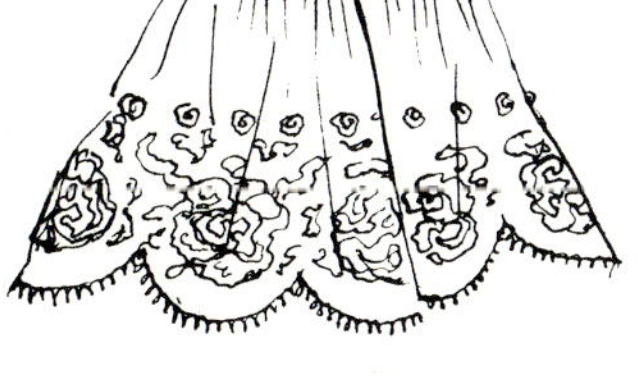

Far left: **Nightdress in heavy satin and real lace from The White House.**

Left: **Silk and lace bedspread and pillows from The White House.**

Below: **Silk hand-embroidered sheets trimmed with real lace from The White House.**

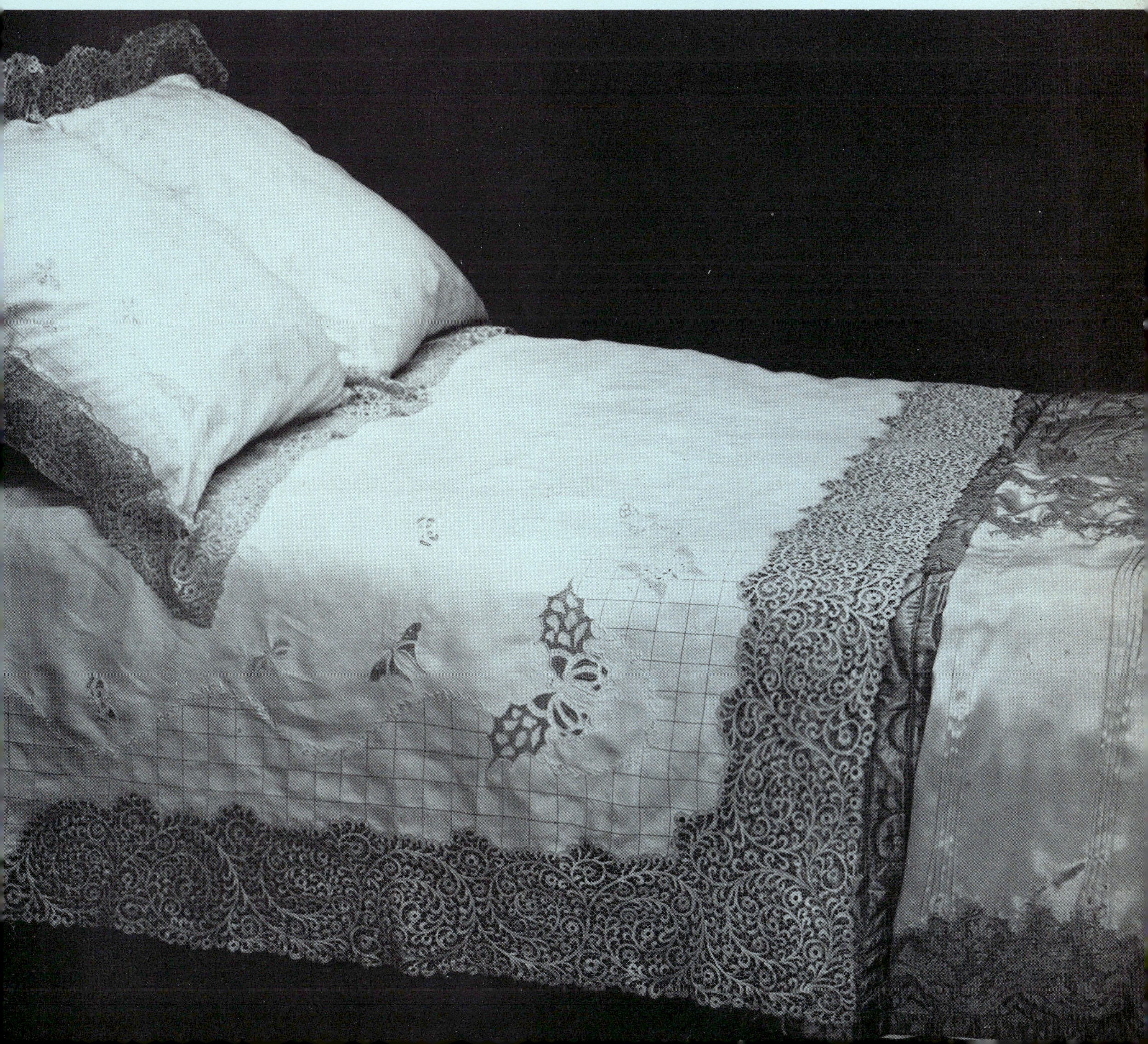

The Veil

A Jewish wedding in Frankfurt-am-Main circa 1866. The bride and groom wear clothes used for special occasions with marriage girdles and are covered by a prayer shawl and canopy from Oppenheim. Drawing by P. Stevenson

The bridal veil has its origins in the *flammeum* or large yellow veil that was used in Greek and Roman times completely to envelop the bride. This symbol of the bride's modesty and perhaps her mystery has remained with us, although the veil has become flimsier and of a more decorative nature. In some cases the veil covers the bride's face during the ceremony and is only thrown back as she leaves the church. The Jewish bride and groom are married beneath a canopy and in some parts of Europe a veil is held over Catholic couples as they kneel at the altar, as a symbol of the Church's blessing of their union. The veil is often accompanied by some type of headdress, generally in the form of a wreath or coronet, and in many countries an elaborate crown is worn. It is customary in the Orthodox Church for a crown to be held over the head of each of the bridal pair, almost in the form of a halo, perhaps to remind the couple that they have many examples of virtue and humility to follow among the saints.

Other headdresses tend to confirm that the veil was once connected with an ancient Eastern rite dedicated to the Goddess of Fertility. Wreaths of orange buds, flowers and even fruit have been worn, and one arrangement shows the veil secured by a gilt or silver wreath of vertical ears of wheat.

a.

(a) **A way to arrange a veil covering the face but leaving the top of the head uncovered. The veil falls in points to the shoulders.**/*Femina*

(b) **Two veil arrangements, circa 1920.**

(c) **A lace veil worn in the Spanish style over a comb covered with flowers, circa 1920.**/*Femina*

(d) **A veil edged with pearls and secured by a headdress of interlaced ribbons and pearls, circa 1920.**/*Femina*

(e) **A lace veil for short hair, held in place by a flowered bandeau.**/*Femina*

(f) **The hairdresser arranges the veil, while the bridesmaids look on.**/*Gazette du Bon Ton*

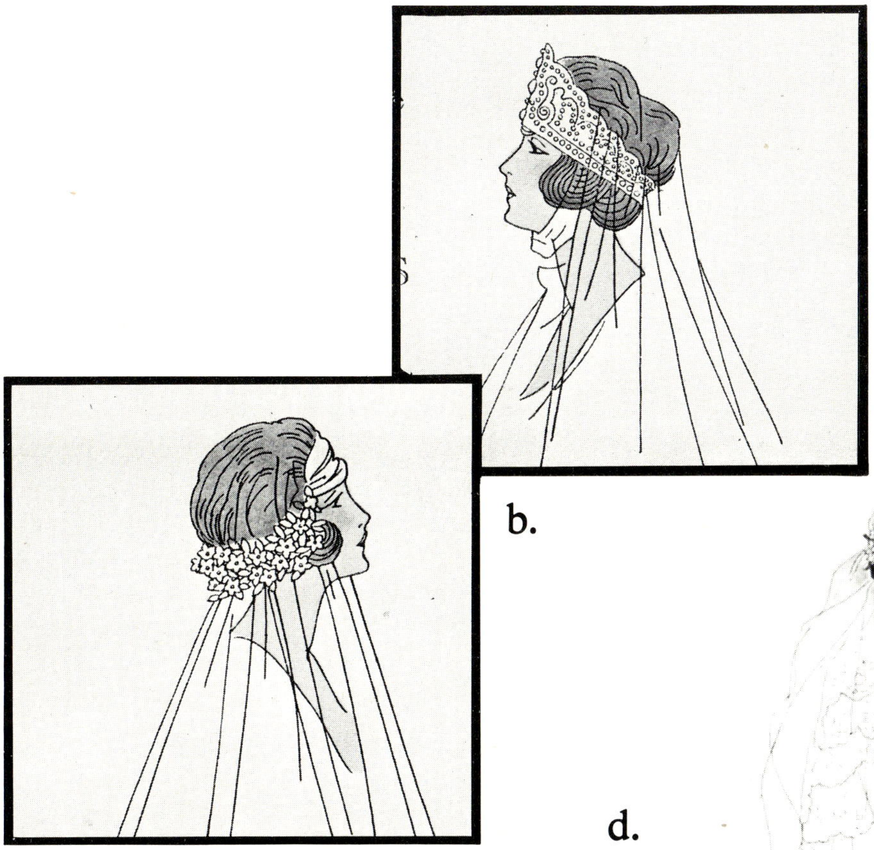

b.

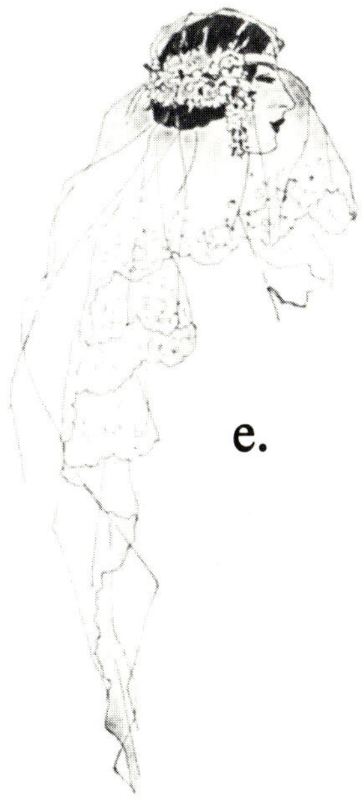

e.

d.

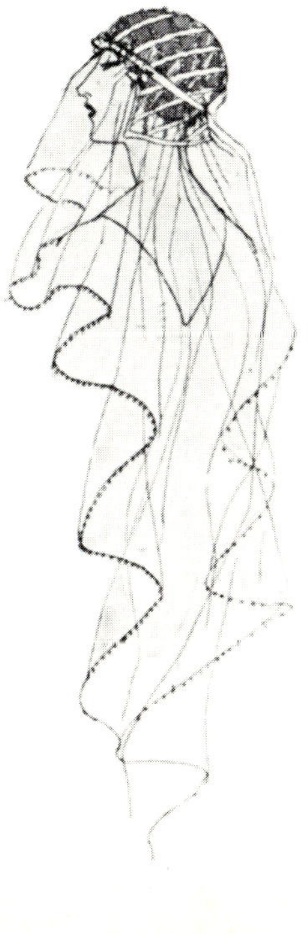

c.

f.

(a) **Veil arrangement, circa 1920.**/*Gazette du Bon Ton*

(b) **A circlet of ears of wheat, probably made in gilt or silver, holds this thin veil in place.**/*Gazette du Bon Ton*

(c) **Veil arrangement, circa 1920.**/*Gazette du Bon Ton*

(d) **A Grecian-style headdress.**/*Gazette du Bon Ton*

(e) **A bridal veil decorated with orange flowers and fruit.**/*Gazette du Bon Ton*

(f) **This beautiful lace veil sets off the extreme simplicity of the satin dress with which it is worn.**/*Femina*

(g) **Orange buds and fine pleated frills decorate this attractive veil arrangement.**/*Gazette du Bon Ton*

(h) **The feather and softly draped veil give this arrangement an oriental look.**/*Gazette du Bon Ton*

a.

b.

d.

e.

c.

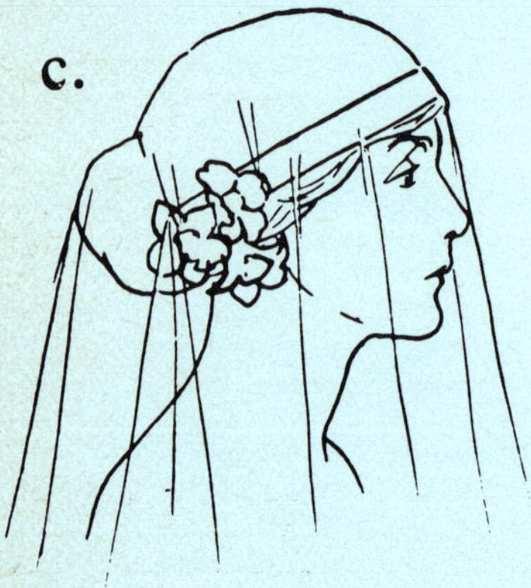

g.

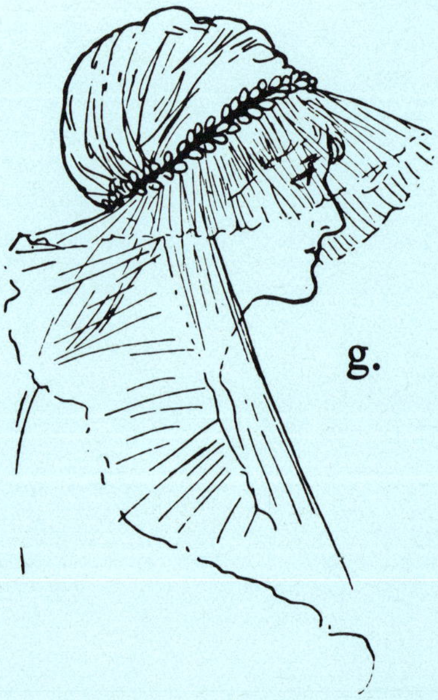

h.

f.

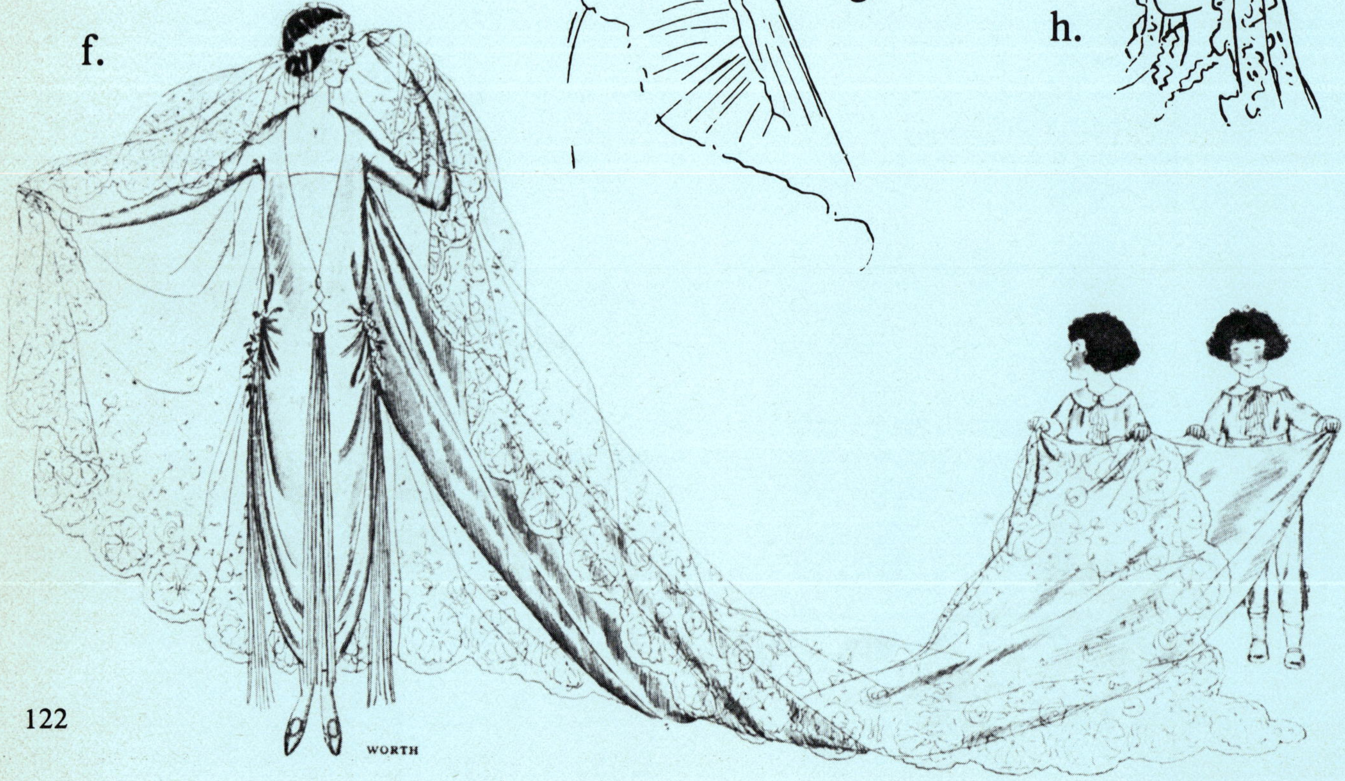

The Ring

'With this ring I thee wed'

The giving of a ring to mark betrothal was an old Roman custom. The ring was probably meant as a mere pledge that the contract would be fulfilled. In Pliny's time conservative custom demanded a simple iron ring, for gold inferred superiority of position, but the gold ring was introduced in the course of the 2nd century. This use of the ring, which was of purely secular origin, eventually received ecclesiastical sanction, and formulae of benediction of the ring exist from the 11th century. In France a priest was required at the betrothal ceremony to witness the exchange of rings, and among the peasantry the place of rings was taken by a coin which was broken in half, the couple taking a piece each. The exact stages by which the wedding ring developed from the betrothal ring can no longer be traced. Gold marriage rings enriched with niello engraving are in existence dating from the 5th century, but it is not certain whether they were incorporated in the actual marriage ceremony.

The museums hold examples of old double and triple rings which turn on a pivot and seem to be a link with the French peasant betrothal custom of sharing a broken coin. It was the custom to separate the rings at the betrothal, which generally took place in front of a witness, the two parties keeping the upper and lower rings and the witness keeping the central ring. When the marriage contract was finally ratified the three rings were joined together again and used for the ceremony.

It is the fashion today for matching engagement and wedding rings to be bought at the time of the engagement and it is possible for the bridegroom to have a wedding ring which matches that of his bride.

Above: **The wedding ring was not always worn on the 3rd finger of the left hand. Drawing by P. Stevenson.**

Below, far left and centre: **Buying the ring.**/*Mary Evans Picture Library*

Below: **A triple ring shown opened out and closed, and a motto ring. Drawing by P. Stevenson.**

Bottom left: **Engagement rings by Prestige.**/*De Beers Diamond Mines Ltd*

Bottom right: **A matching wedding and engagement ring and matching jewellery designed by Leo and Ginnie de Vroomen.**/*De Beers Diamond Mines Ltd*

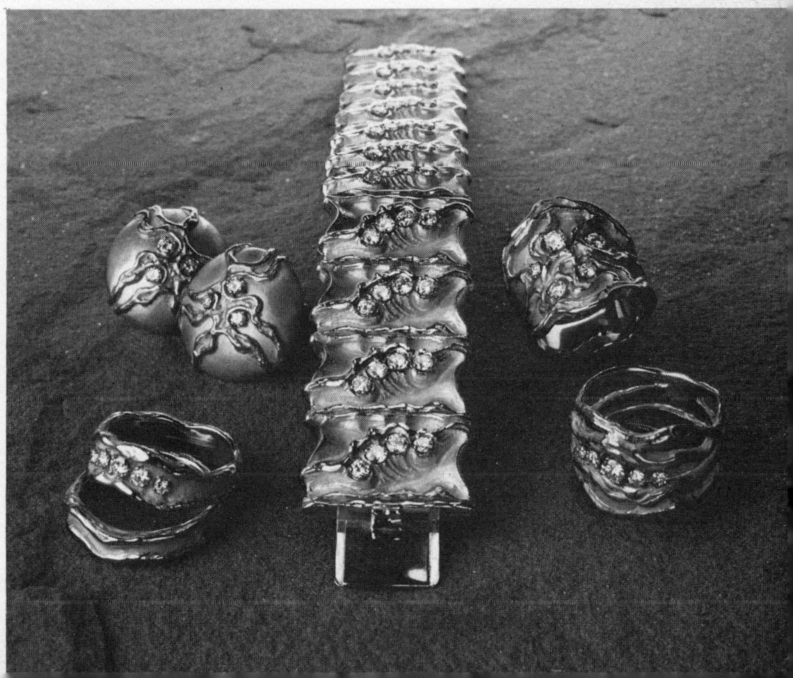

The Cake

Right: **The Silver Wedding cake made for King George VI and Queen Elizabeth, now the Queen Mother, by McVitie & Price Ltd, Harlesden, for the festivities on 26 April 1948.**/*United Biscuits Ltd*

Centre right: **Currants were sent especially for this cake from the girls of Greece. It was made by McVitie and Price Ltd, Harlesden, for the wedding of Princess Marina of Greece on 29 November 1934.**/*United Biscuits Ltd*

Far right: **The wedding cake of Princess Elizabeth (Queen Elizabeth II). The ingredients were a present from the Girl Guides of Australia, brandy from South Africa, rum from Jamaica. The wedding was in November 1947 and the country was still restricted by rationing. It was made by McVitie & Price, Harlesden.**/*United Biscuits Ltd*

Although it was usual to eat Bride Cake at weddings, the elaborate white iced confections we know today seem of fairly recent derivation. An old recipe which may date from Elizabethan times describes how one should put the rich cake mixture into three layers with 'sweetmeats' between each layer; but what these sweetmeats were is a mystery. The idea of having a white iced cake for a wedding is supposed to have originated with Queen Victoria, who asked Messrs Gunters to make her a special decorated wedding cake covered with white icing. This was done and displayed in their shop window and thousands flocked to see it. Since then the white iced wedding cake has been the focal point at the wedding reception.

Right: A wedding cake made in Dresden by Erich Weber for the American and English market probably in the early 20th century. The dome shape represents the bridal veil, and the white iced roses interspersed with real myrtle represent the bridal wreath. The white sugar doves resting on cushions of rose marzipan are interspersed with preserved greengages rolled in sugar and framed in whorls of icing. Around the base are wedges of glazed icing wafers on top of which are arranged white flowers and green leaves of icing sugar. The whole cake is covered with a brilliant glaze of icing sugar and egg whites. Drawing by P. Stevenson.

Below: The wedding cake made by McVitie & Price for Princess Margaret in 1960./*United Biscuits Ltd*

Below right: A wedding cake evidently made for the marriage of two dancing partners./*Barnaby's Picture Library*

2000 A.D. ?

Far left: **A crownless hat with beads and ribbons and a long printed scarf over head and shoulders accompanied by a fan brightly painted with geometric shapes.** ***2000 AD*** **by José van Schaik.**

Left: **A wedding wig of black hair with loops of brightly coloured wools and plaits and curls around the face and neck.** ***2000 AD*** **by José van Schaik.**

Below, far left: **A wedding wig with brightly-coloured ribbons, strings of beads, and tassels attached to combs placed at the side of the head. The broad-collared wedding gown is accompanied by a stick with multi-coloured ribbons and bells to replace the traditional bouquet.** ***2000 AD*** **by José van Schaik.**

Below left: **A dress for the future designed and drawn by Francis Yapp.**

Below: **A dress, designed and drawn by Howard Tangye, in gossamer thread shaped like a cocoon, and just as flexible. It is patterned and jewelled like a dewy spiders web giving complete freedom of movement but completely enveloping the bride. It is worn over a body stocking of shimmering fabric, and the hair is covered by a jewelled hair net. The cocoon is entered by a small opening in the back which stretches wide and closes again.**

Below: Using the peacock as its theme, this dress is in clover pink and white panne velvet and satin and is worn with an embroidered turban. It fits tightly to the knees and then flares out and its wide sleeves, embroidered with white scallops, lead back to a high collar. The whole design of the front of the dress works towards the embroidered satin peacock. The bird's fanned tail forms the bodice of the dress while the bottom of the dress flares from between its feet; even the tightly-fitted rounded shape of the skirt follows the contours of the peacock's body. Designed and drawn by Teresa Noble.

Bottom: The rear view of a wedding dress, slim-fitting and strapless in white patterned satin with an off-the-shoulder cape in silk chiffon. The organdie and satin appliqué embroidery on the back is in the form of a peacock. The dress is worn with an embroidered cloche hat. Designed and drawn by Teresa Noble.

Below: Dress designed and drawn by Stella Brooks who says: "By 2000AD I believe marriages will take place only to produce offspring and for this a limited number of government permits will be issued to couples found both physically and mentally sound. By 2000 the tension and pace of life will have made sterility an all too common problem and couples fortunate enough to obtain permits to procreate will be so anxious to do so that the marriage ceremony will become more and more a fertility rite."

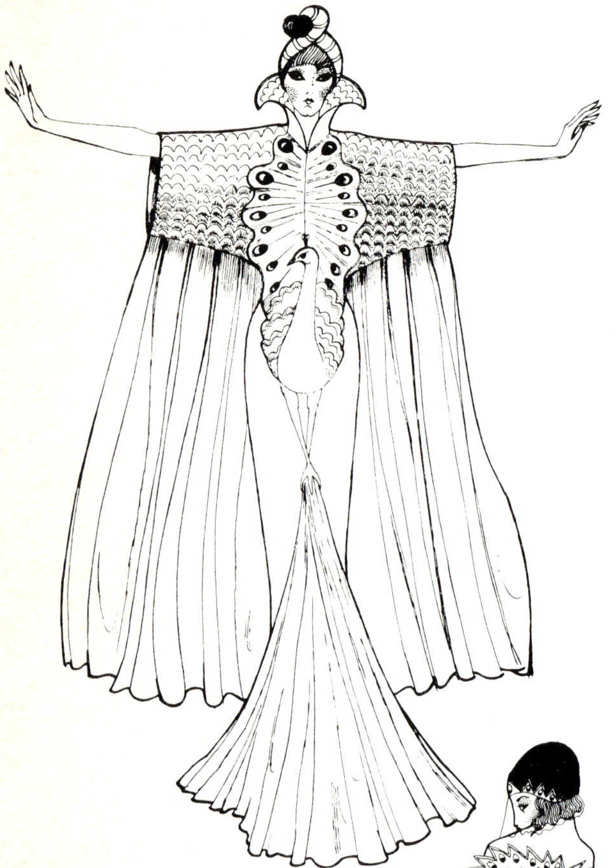

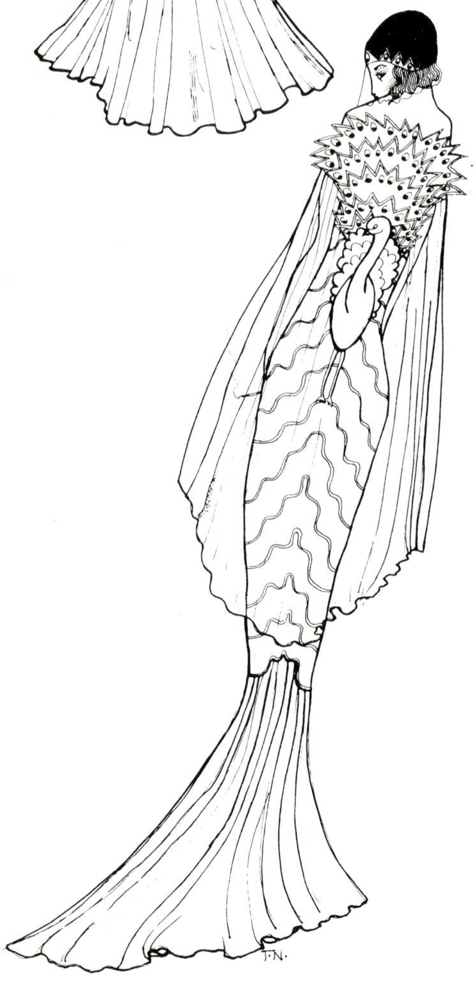